THE SOWER AND THE SEED

THE SOWER AND THE SEED
Reflections on the Development of Consciousness

Alan Mulhern

Illustrated by Lindsey C. Harris

Routledge
Taylor & Francis Group
LONDON AND NEW YORK

First published 2015 by Karnac Books Ltd.

Published 2018 by Routledge
2 Park Square, Milton Park, Abingdon, Oxon OX14 4RN
711 Third Avenue, New York, NY 10017, USA

Routledge is an imprint of the Taylor & Francis Group, an informa business

British Library Cataloguing in Publication Data

A C.I.P. for this book is available from the British Library

ISBN-13: 9781782202462 (pbk)

Typeset by V Publishing Solutions Pvt Ltd., Chennai, India

CONTENTS

ACKNOWLEDGEMENTS ix

ABOUT THE AUTHOR xi

PREFACE xiii

COMMENTS BY THE ILLUSTRATOR xvii

INTRODUCTION xxi

PART I: ORIGINS, BECOMING, AND EMERGENCE

CHAPTER ONE
Origins 4

CHAPTER TWO
Becoming 10

CHAPTER THREE
The emergence of human consciousness 14

PART II: CONSCIOUSNESS EMERGING FROM NATURE

CHAPTER FOUR
The good mother 30

CHAPTER FIVE
Fertility and power 34

CHAPTER SIX
Earth's terror 40

CHAPTER SEVEN
The opposites at the root of consciousness 44

CHAPTER EIGHT
The Book of Job 50

CHAPTER NINE
Dragon fight 60

PART III: SEPARATION: THE RISE AND FALL OF CONSCIOUSNESS

CHAPTER TEN
The emergence of civilisation 68

CHAPTER ELEVEN
The Garden of Eden 78

CHAPTER TWELVE
Lucifer 84

CHAPTER THIRTEEN
Banishment 90

PART IV: THE FALLEN AND THE HIGHER STATES OF HUMANITY

CHAPTER FOURTEEN
The fallen state 102

CHAPTER FIFTEEN
Isis, Osiris, and Seth 106

CHAPTER SIXTEEN
Evil and the shadow 112

CHAPTER SEVENTEEN
The higher self 122

CHAPTER EIGHTEEN
The experience of love 126

PART V: THE ENLIGHTENMENT AND CAPITALIST PROJECT

INTRODUCTION
The scientific revolution and capitalism 134

CHAPTER NINETEEN
The source of the achievements of capitalism 137

CHAPTER TWENTY
Capitalism as crisis 140

CHAPTER TWENTY-ONE
How has consciousness changed with capitalism? 147

CHAPTER TWENTY-TWO
Death potential in consciousness 154

PART VI: THE QUEST

The individual journey of The Quest 164

APPENDIX ONE 211

APPENDIX TWO 215

APPENDIX THREE 217

APPENDIX FOUR 219

GLOSSARY 221

REFERENCES 233

INDEX 237

ACKNOWLEDGEMENTS

I wish to give heartfelt thanks to Lindsey Harris, a colleague who works as a Jungian analyst in London. She has provided forty-four wonderful original illustrations for the book, which have been an inspiration and enormous help with its completion. She has also provided countless suggestions and most helpful advice. Her capacity to attune to the underlying message of the text and provide powerful, mythological, and archetypal images that express the inner meaning in visual form has been extraordinary. Far beyond the call of duty she has given detailed feedback on my attempts at verse and has extensively helped with the reading and editing of the text. The philosophy expressed in these pages is, of course, my own, but Lindsey has been most tactful in those areas where agreement has not been unanimous. Without this quality in her this book may not have come into being—and certainly not in its present format.

We wish to thank the following (in alphabetical order) for their generous support in the reading of the text, providing feedback, as well as giving encouragement and inspiration: Martin Bates, Nadya Berlin, Jack Bierschenk, Anne Baring, Carol Clapham, Jim Dening, Mark Dunn, Patrick Drury, Michael Hession, Cynthia Morrison, Melanie Mulhern, Gill Stuart, Susan Taylor, Kevin Wilson.

This project is inspired by the tradition of analytical psychology. The works of C. G. Jung and Eric Neumann's The *Origin and History of Consciousness* (1989) have been foundational to the project. Of especial inspiration have been the writings of Anne Baring. Her recent *The Dream of the Cosmos: A Quest for the Soul* (2013) was a guiding light throughout.

Text and poems are by Alan Mulhern. Illustrations are by Lindsey Harris.

ABOUT THE AUTHOR

Alan Mulhern trained as a Jungian psychotherapist and has worked for thirty years in private practice in London. He was also an academic economist. He has given numerous workshops in the UK and in Venezuela on subjects such as dream analysis, narcissism, the shadow, psychoanalytic diagnosis, and healing in psychotherapy. He has written on the subject of the changes in the profession of psychotherapy in the modern age. The nature of healing intelligence is of especial interest.

PREFACE

This book was initially conceived as a slim volume illustrating the path of psychotherapy and self-awareness. However, the seed grew into a much larger enterprise to include over forty illustrations, numerous poems, and six major sections with a text ambitiously attempting an account of the origins, development, and current dilemmas of human consciousness. Its methodology is to use a combination of text, illustrations, and poems in the contemplative and spiritual tradition.

Both I and the illustrator are Jungian psychotherapists and therefore this project is strongly influenced by the traditions of our discipline as well as by decades of work with clients. Experience in the *deep psyche* was indispensable for the project. In addition to a psychological and mythological perspective there is also a strong metaphysical line cast through the book especially in its motifs of *immanence* and *creative destruction*.

I am also an economist and have spent many decades in the university lecture hall. I am aware of the powerful economic and political forces that have shaped modern consciousness and have led to its current impasse. Chapter Five, for example, focuses on the Enlightenment and capitalism.

The project was not *intellectually* preconceived but driven essentially by inspiration, readily observed in the numerous illustrations and poems that hopefully communicate their message aesthetically. Metaphysical expression rapidly runs up against the limits of language and is forced to find other pathways of expression that embody feelings and higher intuition. For example, this inspiration, specifically, was found in a muse, Isis, the Ancient Egyptian goddess. Most psychotherapists would say that muses are intuitive faculties symbolised in imaginary figures. I have no problem with this formulation except to say that I, like many children, writers, musicians, and, I admit, the psychologically distressed, need to treat such figures as *real*. Thus, by way of example, at one point, I found myself talking to Isis about a problem in the book (yes, my neighbours have long regarded me with suspicion) and the answer I received was that I should write poems for at least every chapter or section. I replied that thirty or so poems were beyond my reach since in my life I had written precisely none. She indicated that it would not be a problem and that I should have no fear or hesitation. I will leave it to the reader to judge the appropriateness of listening to inner voices. Thus, the book became reshaped from its original vision. I could give fifty similar examples but the point is made.

The poems and illustrations were constructed in an interchange between the illustrator, Lindsey Harris, and myself. Sometimes the poem came first, at other times the illustration. Frequently, the image or the poem would be half formulated and there would be a back and forth exchange until both were complete and complementary. The illustrations arose from the mythological and spiritual background that permeates the Jungian tradition. The text also came primarily from inner inspirational sources. For example, I had little idea, when we began, that the opening chapters would express a metaphysical theory of *immanence*. Thus, the book was not formulated in advance but, true to the impulse of immanence, *emerged* into being. Moreover, the text also owes its style to such sources. It is highly compact, at times to the point of enigma. It largely dispenses with enticing introductions, ample explanations, well-rounded conclusions, attractive case studies, and comparisons with other works. It often declares rather than argues its points—reminiscent of Taoist or Hindu texts. This was because a voice continually whispered in my ear "… only the essence". Thus, there was a strong impulse to condense until the meaning *felt* right and it resonated with the inner world, rather than to present long reasoned argument. It felt much better, given the style of the book, to be declaratory rather than argumentatively persuasive, to say concisely what the core of my experience was, and not to shelter behind other authors and schools. It felt right that the heart and intuition—spirit—should lead and the intellect follow.

It is often remarked that a better performance in music, sport, or theatre is given when the participants put aside their intense training and enter fully into the moment, the living present. The same could be said for a psychotherapy session or even the writing of some books—such as this. However, when one surfaces and reflects upon one's training and background one recognises the antecedents that have made it all possible. Thus, there is a long history underlying every idea one has wrestled with. It has all been said before and is all being said now. For example, there is an immense devotional literature in all the religious traditions; there is a mystical literature of the *path, quest*, or *pilgrimage* that has inspired so much music, opera, theatre, literature, spiritual texts, and visual arts. Consider the impact of the Grail Legend in the Western tradition as one example, or the stories of pilgrimage in the world's spiritual literature. There are scientists of mystical persuasion, such as Teilhard de Chardin and David Bohm, who have presented outstanding visions in the twentieth century of how our material universe has emerged from a deeper reality and intelligence. There are remarkable contemporary writers, such as Capra and Baring, who have presented astonishing breadth of vision and compelling arguments on these themes. There is an abundance of poetry, painting, and illustration that has inspired countless artists to contribute their vision of the *journey*. The *Avatamsaka Sutra* in the Buddhist tradition and Dante's *Divine Comedy* are two outstanding examples. Individual mystics such as Hildegard of Bingen, William Blake, and Carl Jung in the West as well as countless Hindu, Buddhist and Taoist devotees, including the Buddha himself, have devoted their lives to expressing a vision of how human consciousness, trapped in a lower egoic existence, can find a path to an enlightened and higher consciousness.

The exception to this "inspirational" style, led by intuition, feeling, and aesthetics, is Chapter Five on the Enlightenment and capitalism. The reader will notice a change to a more analytic, argued, and rational presentation—not inappropriate, as it happens, for the object under scrutiny, the age of science and materialism.

The final section, "The Quest", returns to form and abandons argument, presenting a narrative consisting of poems, illustrations, and a limited psychological commentary of the pilgrimage, the journey to a transcendental centre of meaning and experience that lies at the core of human consciousness.

COMMENTS BY THE ILLUSTRATOR

I am grateful to Alan Mulhern for having given me the opportunity to illustrate this book. The project has grown in an organic way from small beginnings in 2012 to what eventually became this extended series of pictures.

Each picture had its individual beginning in the seed of one of the author's ideas or poems. From a blank paper and a pencil, and a trust in the unconscious processes in the deeper psyche, each illustration grew and evolved, almost of its own accord, through early sketches to a final rough, and only later being consciously worked up. The basic constraints were black and white only and mostly upright format for the book page. The materials were rough pencil drawings to begin with, followed by later working in pen and ink, fine-liners, gouache paints, and watercolour washes. Digital photographs of each stage of every illustration were emailed to the author to ensure the picture was becoming a fitting complement to the text.

Visual art has an immediate impact and is easily accessible to the eye. Some of these illustrations contain a narrative or mythological motifs of a story with a hidden meaning. Though the story is conveyed in a simple pictorial manner, there are sometimes mysteries under the surface. This is because there is always another world beyond the literal everyday one. Whether one calls this the Jungian world of the archetypes, or the daimonic realm, the collective mythological unconscious, the kingdom of heaven, or the land of the fairies, it is there, and I wish that something of this other world be revealed though these illustrations.

Certain of the illustrations are based upon a circular structure, which links them to the ancient Sanskrit mandala form or sacred circle. C. G. Jung understood the mandala as an expression of the psyche in its totality, or as a potential for wholeness, or at least a containment of certain ideas or psychological states which might otherwise be fragmented or disparate. The mandala therefore holds together on the page a numinous power, offering the observer a chance to meditate upon something beyond the everyday, and which is full of unknown mystery and awe. I hope that some of the illustrations capture the profound ideas that are expressed in the author's text, and perhaps pin them down, however fleetingly, within a single image. As Jung said, "It is as if we did not know, or continually forgot, that everything of which we are conscious is an image, and that image is psyche" (Collected Works 13, par. 75).

There have been numerous influences along the way, which I list briefly; the beautiful medieval books of hours and illuminated manuscripts, stained glass windows, sacred geometry, Celtic art, alchemical illustrations such as the *Rosarium Philosophorum*, the *Splendor Solis*, and other seventeenth century alchemical engravings, the illustrations of Hildegard of Bingen, William Blake, and Gustav Doré, *The Red Book* of C. G. Jung, Hindu and ancient Egyptian art, as well as numerous medieval and Renaissance paintings and art work. Readers may enjoy spotting the many deliberate echoes of earlier artists' work, to whom I pay silent homage. Indeed I have drawn upon my abiding love and knowledge of art history and feel honoured to count myself a humble follower in a great tradition of esoteric drawing.

Lindsey C. Harris

Figure 1.
Mother of all in you we trust, this world evolved from soul.
From stars to earth and earth to stars, such glory we behold.

INTRODUCTION

The purpose of this book is to explore human consciousness from the perspective of consciousness itself. What has the psyche to say about its own origins and development? An impossible task? Surely we need an objective account of consciousness, a scientific investigation? This may be possible for some parts of consciousness but not for its experiential nature. It would be like asking individuals to give an objective account of their lives, their feelings of being born, or falling in love. Consciousness, however, is inevitably bound up with itself. Try looking at yourself in a mirror objectively. Nevertheless, expression of ourselves is possible, as is our projection into external narratives or even abstract symbols such as painting or music. The collective, as well as the individual, can express itself in a similar manner, for instance through creation myths, scriptures, metaphysical speculations, religious rituals, and legends. The essence seeks it expression. The soul needs to be known.

Part I explores the origins of consciousness from a mytho-psychological angle based on the view that consciousness projects itself into creation myths. The concept of *immanence* is the underlying philosophy of this book, that a vast intelligence is *within* the evolutionary process. It is beyond the good, the benign, or any moral projection we put into it. It is presented here, as Shiva in Hindu philosophy, as a combination of opposites, a process of *creative destruction*, a cosmic principle and therefore manifest in nature, all life forms, human nature, and even societies. In this sense, all life and human consciousness is an evolution of this creative destructive spirit which manifests and evolves higher orders of complexity, intelligence, and consciousness—and then dissolves them. This section also presents a summary account of human nature using a mixture of Jungian analytical psychology plus our knowledge of the evolution of the human brain from palaeoanthropological studies.

Part II presents the first early stage of human psyche as it is immersed in nature and the realm of the Great Mother. The themes of fertility and power, applicable to all life forms, saturate the history of humanity, most evidently in this period stretching roughly from 40,000 years ago up to the birth of modern civilisations.

Part III shows the transition to patriarchal religious consciousness (Judaism, Islam, and Christianity, for example) and its world view. This is dramatically captured by the myths of the killing of the dragon or the bull fight whereby a violent separation form the world of nature takes place. These religions, which shaped humanity in the Near East and the West, decisively altered world history. This was a necessary development of the individuation of the species—though at a cost.

Part IV examines the origins of evil and goodness in human beings. It uses myths from the Hebrew bible, Ancient Egypt, and Greece to do this. Are there constants in human nature in spite of these large scale transitions in human consciousness? Besides the five evolved structural layers of our nature outlined in Part I, the universal theme across all traditions is that the transition to consciousness is inherently problematic since it creates a separation from the realm of nature and instinct. Our ego consciousness, although emerging around 200,000 years ago with *Homo sapiens* (and greater brain size) nevertheless developed over time right up to the birth of modern civilisations where it became more robust and "separated". This "rise" of consciousness out of nature and its "fall" or separation into a separated egoic state is its central dilemma.

Part IV illustrates the great change in consciousness with the emergence and development of capitalism. The Enlightenment and scientific revolution, essential for capitalism to evolve, needed a special change in consciousness provided for by Protestantism in Northern Europe and later the United States. The other main religions such as Catholicism, Islam, Hinduism, Confucianism, Buddhism, or Taoism, were unfavourable to the development of this type of economic system and although many of the civilisations within them had many ingredients necessary for capitalism, they lacked the essential contributions of Protestantism. However, capitalism is destined to undermine all religions and replace them with a thoroughly materialist philosophy. As well as being a profoundly creative system the industrial system, its chief child, is equally destructive and has in recent times produced enough weaponry to wipe out human existence and most of life on earth. A death potential in consciousness is now made very real. It is suggested that humanity will undergo species-trauma in the near future and the remaining human populations will face the choice of fundamental reform or inevitable extinction. Capitalism also presents many changes in consciousness during the stages of its development, including the latest, the digital age, which we term *informational capitalism*, where human consciousness is being aligned to and even fused with artificial intelligence.

Part VI—no matter what the situation in the collective, the path for individual progress and even enlightenment is open to individuals. "The Quest" presents a series of illustrations, poems, and short text that illustrate the search of the individual on the path of higher consciousness. The metaphor of the pilgrimage is used and shows essential psychological as well as spiritual steps on such a journey.

PART I

ORIGINS, BECOMING, AND EMERGENCE

Creation myths deal with basic puzzles such as how the world began and what is mankind's place in it. This book is no different. It attempts to combine ancient wisdom with findings of modern science, for example, those of cosmology, evolution, and palaeo-anthropology, and tells an old story of a vast intelligence that has created but also evolved the cosmos and all its life forms, including ourselves. Like all creation myths the narrative rapidly centres on mankind's consciousness and moral dilemmas. Part I is divided into three chapters.

The first, "Origins", contemplates the beginning of things and gazes, as it were, at the night sky, at a universe that began 13.8 billion years ago and is still expanding. Inevitably, into its starry mirror we project ourselves. Human consciousness is part of that which it observes. Part I suggests a primal intelligence or spirit that manifests itself through the material universe and ourselves.

The second, "Becoming", outlines the creative-destructive process that, we argue, evolves all matter and life. It suggests, as Heraclitus and the Taoists did, that the universe is in constant change, and moreover there have been countless universes, for the cosmos is eternal, as the Hindus have believed for thousands of years. Life and intelligence are not accidental to this evolving creation but are at its core. In particular, human intelligence is its evolved, living spirit.

The third, "The emergence of human consciousness", provides a summary view of human nature, strongly influenced by palaeoanthropology and the school of Jungian psychology, which has evolved from the animal world through hominids to *Homo sapiens* who emerged in Africa a mere 200,000 years ago. Five evolved interrelated layers of our nature are outlined: animal inheritance, emotional structure, ego consciousness, the unconscious, and a higher consciousness, held together by an intelligence, called by Jung the archetype of the Self, an expression of the integrated intelligence of the life process itself. Thus, human nature evolves from an underlying intelligence. The purpose of human consciousness, it is suggested, is to fulfil all parts of our nature and to unite with this intelligence.

CHAPTER ONE

Origins

Something formless yet complete,
Precedes both man and earth.
It lay outside of space and time,
It had no death or birth.
It did exist before this world,
All things it does bring forth.
It is the mother of all life,
The father of all thought.

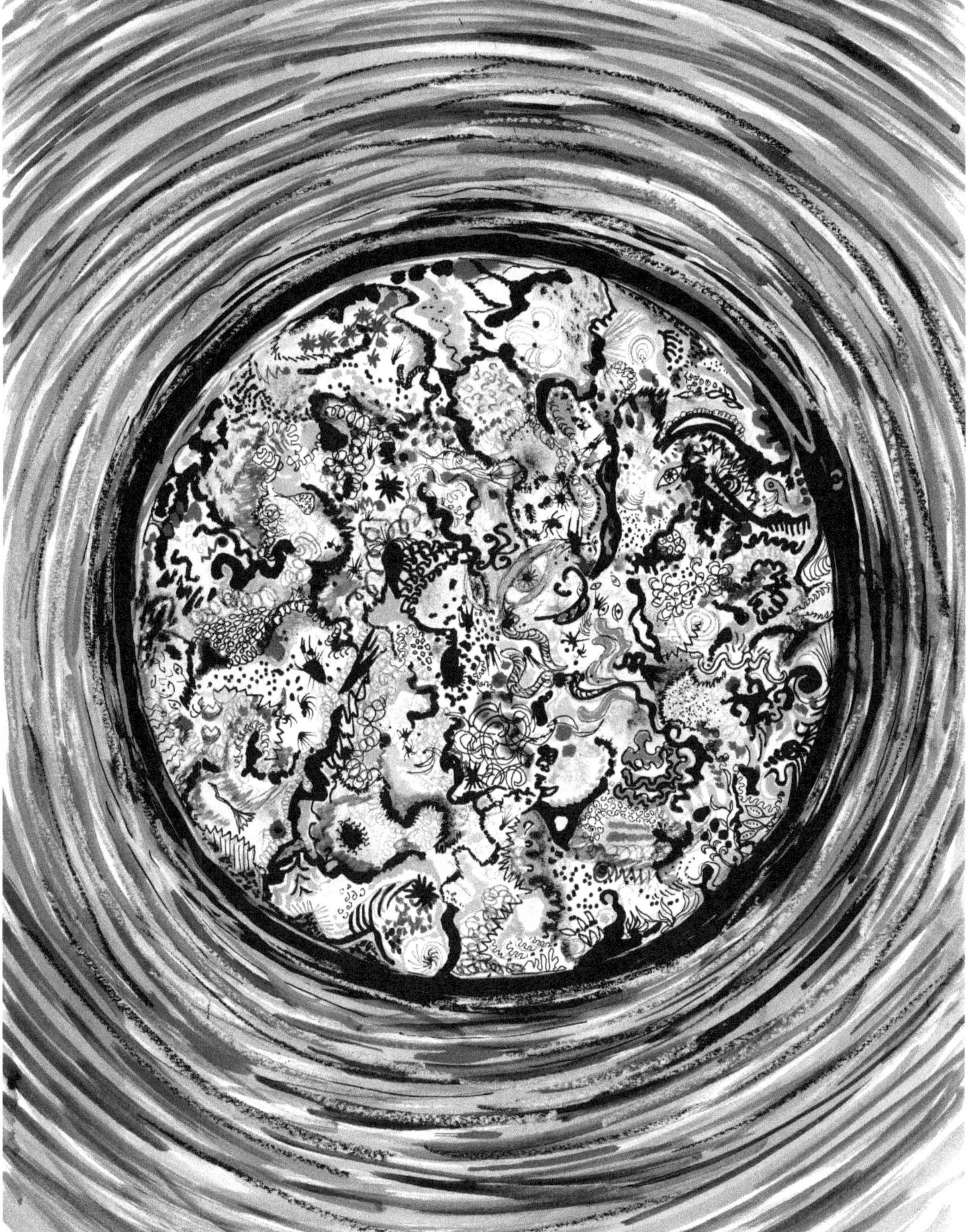

Figure 2. Origins.

Human beings long for harmony within themselves, a sense of meaning and belonging in the cosmos. In the mirror of the starry firmament we find the creative-destructive nature of our own psyche. We also sense, and are thrilled at, the wholeness that underlies these opposites—an integrative intelligence that permeates all things including the depths of our own nature.

Our consciousness is compelled to look at the preconscious state and divine its nature. Symbols of the totality, found in all cultures and epochs, intimate that once, before time, the universe was one; that despite the problematic entrance of consciousness there was, is, and shall be a unity to the cosmos. There is a longing and intuition that the conflicted human being, consisting of so many parts, derives from and can return to a unity outside ego consciousness.

The uroborus, (see Figure 2), the serpent with its tail in its mouth, symbolises the self-contained nature of the totality. This mythological, original state is a union of opposites, light and dark, positive and negative, the state before creation. It therefore transcends consciousness, giving an intuitive, symbolic form to a preconscious condition outside of time, space, causality, and the duality of existence in which the opposites are contained. Here, we may contemplate symbolically the beginning of things, the world, all life, and ourselves. It refers to an original self-contained circle, where all opposites are united. Plato intimates: "Therefore the demiurge made the world in the shape of a sphere, giving it the figure which of all is the most perfect and the most equal to itself." (in Sallis, 1999).

There are various points of contact with such an image-symbol. It represents:

A primal intuition that there is an essence that encompasses all things, a foundation of everything, a force that is omnipresent through the material and non-material world, that underlies both the human self and nature.

A pre-dawn symbol of the state of humanity before the birth of consciousness.

A symbol of existence in our mothers' womb and infancy before the formation of ego.

A mandala symbol that occurs in spiritual, mystic, and artistic states as an image of wholeness, healing the fragmentation of the psyche. It arises spontaneously in children's drawings, dreams, and trance states of all peoples.

A supreme goal of consciousness which is to strive to end the struggle of opposites that constitute human existence. It is an intuitive representation of transcendence.

Alpha and omega, since it prefigures the state after consciousness when all opposites are reduced back to a unity. It is therefore a symbol of death and a transpersonal wholeness transcending the state of individuals or indeed the species.

By perceiving a unity in the original state, we sense the wholeness of the cosmos, a unity of all things—including ourselves. Since human beings are from the earth, which in turn evolved from the universe, an identity should exist between mankind and the cosmos. While this must be true physically, for example that the carbon atoms of the early universe are required for the carbon in our bodies, it also hints at a psychological and spiritual dimension. Our basic identity with the cosmos is what we have always longed for instead of experiencing ourselves as baffled observers or alien intrusions.

Modern science has discovered that the immense galaxy, within which the earth is situated, consists of hundreds of billions of stars, not to mention their planets. But our galaxy is only one amongst hundreds of billions of others across the visible universe. All this is only a small fraction of the dark matter and energy that fills the apparent void. Since the expansion of the universe can be measured, its beginning can be dated to *circa* 13.8 billion years ago, presumably to a state of heat and compression in some sense equal to the force of the expansion to follow. Outside this original singularity, black hole, or dark perfect sphere nothing could exist—no time, space, light, energy, or matter. Within it, the totality of the cosmos, *in potentia*, existed. Creation and destruction, matter and spirit were as one. The possibility of all life, and even consciousness, is prefigured here in this alchemical vessel. This matrix expanded very quickly, creating, from the primal energy, the material, form, and time of the still-expanding universe. 4.5 billion years ago our solar system was formed from the gas and matter in this spatial region that contracted under the force of gravity. There is immense propulsion towards the creation of higher order in the evolution of the universe and life. Intelligence is integral to the cosmos. Yet, from beginning to end, it is pitched against destruction, chance, disorder, and death.

Human beings in early civilisations moved beyond their state of immersion in nature to consideration of origins, envisioning gods that created the world. They were at the edges of their consciousness, the most far-flung contemplation and mystical experiences that could help them formulate an idea or articulate an image of the beginnings of all things. This inevitably is a projection of consciousness as it contemplates the conditions of its pre-existence.

The consciousness of modern man has expanded to include evolution, a vast universe evolved over billions of years, a knowledge of physics, chemistry, and biology immensely more advanced than that of the ancient world. Nevertheless, our contemporary theory of origins, in some respects, closely resembles certain intuitions of early civilisations, especially the Hindu, and in a similar manner our psyche projects itself into it and then searches for the impossible—for language that describes the state beyond the opposites which underlies our consciousness. The Rig Veda, written 1500–1000 BC, comments:

Then was not non-existent nor existent:
There was no realm of air, no sky beyond it.
Death was not then, nor was there aught immortal:
No sign was there, the day's and night's divider.
That One Thing, breathless, breathed by its own nature:
Apart from it was nothing whatsoever …

The Gods are later than this world's production.
Who knows then whence it first came into being?
He, the first origin of this creation,
whether he formed it all or did not form it,
Whose eye controls this world in highest heaven,
He verily knows it, or perhaps he knows not.

Rig Veda, Hymn 129: Creation (Griffith, 1896/2009)—see Appendix Three for a more extended text and author's comments.

The astronomer's lens, peering out to the creation of our universe, is human consciousness, like a mirror to its deep centre, forever examining its origins, birth, and even the preconditions of its existence. But ultimate knowledge forever vanishes beyond our scope. In the moment of dating the universe we realise there must be others preceding it; that the cosmos must be infinite and eternal; that there have been endless cycles of creation and dissolution. The intelligence of mankind gazes at the universe only to realise that we are an expression of this infinite intelligence itself. That which we have called God or Brahman we then name cosmos; that which we named cosmos we now call Self. Consciousness and the universe are inextricably linked. One searches for the creator, forever finding oneself.

CHAPTER TWO

Becoming

Creation acts through power divine,
Through destruction life is born.
God rests at centre of the wheel,
Serpent makes the world of form.
Our mother life, our mother death,
All becoming, source of all.
We, thy children, human race,
Seek your wisdom, hear your call.

Figure 3. Becoming.

The cosmos undergoes eternal cycles of creation and dissolution. The world and all its life forms have evolved, but its intelligence or spirit is coexistent with matter and is immanent in this evolution.

The original oneness is beyond all existence but in its unfolding contains the matter, energy, intelligence, and spirit of the whole universe. The original cosmic singularity precedes time, causality, mass, and space and yet is the origin and determiner of all things, the potentiator of our universe, which from the beginning to end of its cycle is an evolving drama of creation and destruction. The impulsion towards higher order, seeded into the cosmos, produces life forms throughout the universe that evolve ever greater degrees of intelligence. These, in turn, are subject to dissolution.

The notion of the evolution of the universe, the earth, and life is now undeniable but it is by no means the whole story. In its current state the theory of evolution neglects the inherent intelligence or spirit, coexistent with matter, that lies in the cosmos and in life. Thus, spirit is *immanent* within matter and evolution. The vehicle of this becoming is an eternal cycle of creative destruction through which higher degrees of intelligence evolve and disintegrate. This view contrasts with the narrow materialist belief that intelligence, life, and consciousness are incidental rather than inherent to the cosmos. It also contrasts with the religious belief in a transcendent god who, as creator of the universe, is somehow outside of creation. The view of immanence expressed here is that intelligence or spirit is *within* creation and is manifested in its development. Evolving intelligence is its expression.

It was commonly believed, up to the recent past, that the earth was the centre of the solar and stellar system, that there was constancy in the heavens and earth, and that this staggering complexity resulted as an act of creation by God. With no idea of the age of the earth there were also serious propositions in the seventeenth century that it was created in 4004 BC (Bishop Usher, 1650). Similarly, in many religions humans believed they were unique and different, the chosen of God; that their reason and consciousness, the gift of a creator, distinguished them from all creatures, making them masters. Just as the earth was centre of the universe, man was the *raison d'être* of creation. The paradigm change in our cosmology and psychology has been revolutionary.

In the twentieth century ego intelligence was displaced from its supposed central position and revolved around the unconscious. The story of evolution is now established and ego intelligence, moreover, is no longer the exclusive feature of *Homo sapiens* but actually preceded him in the *homo* lineage by *Homo neanderthalis* and *Homo erectus* among others (see Appendix One). Primate intelligence is also far more advanced than previously thought. Indeed self-consciousness, the previously supposed exclusive property of humans, exists in certain primates and, probably, other animals. The conclusion is inescapable. Advanced intelligence and even self-consciousness developed in evolution in various animals and hominids; *Homo sapiens* is its inheritor. Intelligence is not exclusive to any species, even our own. It is, rather, inherent within evolution itself.

While the precursors of our consciousness lie in our animal and hominid evolutionary past its origins are in the intelligence of life itself and beyond that in the intelligence of the cosmos. This viewpoint requires a paradigm shift away from a dead and mechanistic universe in which the emergence of life and consciousness are accidents. The alternative vision is that the cosmos is intelligence or spirit itself and has an ordering principle or Logos (see Glossary). Matter is no longer primary but coexistent with spirit. Intelligence precedes *Homo sapiens*, primates, and, indeed, all life forms. It is woven into the cosmos and the emergence of life and consciousness are the expression of it as, indeed, is its evolution into higher forms. The following distinctions are therefore made.

The material world is "manifested" and arises from a deeper source than is apparent to our immediate reason, consciousness, or senses. Such a proposition is not simply mysticism (although it certainly includes that) but is also a coherent interpretation of relativity and quantum theory where the world of matter, space, time, and causation, typical of the world view of classical physics, dissolves and is replaced by an immensely dynamic and powerful, interconnected field of inter-relationships (see Bohm, 1980, and Capra, 1975).

Intelligence lies in the cosmos, in nature and in all life forms. It pre-exists consciousness, which is a later development within life forms. Just as higher degrees of order and intelligence evolved on earth, so they evolve throughout the universe.

As the Hindus intuited thousands of years ago (*Rig Veda, Bhagavata Purana*, Griffith, 1896/2009), there are countless universes following one another. Therefore, on the macro scale, one may think of time as cyclical, with intelligence and evolution in a perpetual cycle of creative destruction. Linear evolution, leading to one absolute and final goal, does not fit with the circular viewpoint. Intelligence does not evolve *de novum*, fresh and original out of evolution. Rather, it is built into the cosmos eternally, has repeatedly arisen in previous universes and is teeming throughout the current one. Intelligence is neither an end point of evolution, or external to life, nor the gift of a personal God, or accidental—it is part of the fabric of nature and evolves into ever higher degrees of order.

Consciousness is concentrated intelligence in the brains of creatures promoting their survival and evolving and manifesting from the inherent intelligence within nature.

Self-awareness is the further development of consciousness particularly characterising human beings, though it began to evolve in other species in the *homo* lineage, as well as existing to a limited though definite extent in certain animals, especially primates. It is the capacity of intelligence to examine itself.

Higher consciousness is transcendent awareness and symbolic communication over and above survival and ego needs.

The Self is an inner directing function of order, growth, and individuation in the human psyche and is a deeper consciousness and intelligence than that of the ego. It is an expression of the integrative wholeness that underlies our bodies and nature. This central ordering principle within the human psyche is a development of the natural ordering process in the cosmos and is evident in all life forms.

From a materialist view human consciousness is ultimately inexplicable. From the metaphysical perspective of immanence it is quite different:

human consciousness is the living spirit of the universe.

CHAPTER THREE

The emergence of human consciousness

The birth of human consciousness,
A very recent spark,
Evolving as a mystery,
A light within the dark.
It is a part of nature,
To past it does connect,
But looking to the heavens,
Our instincts it rejects.

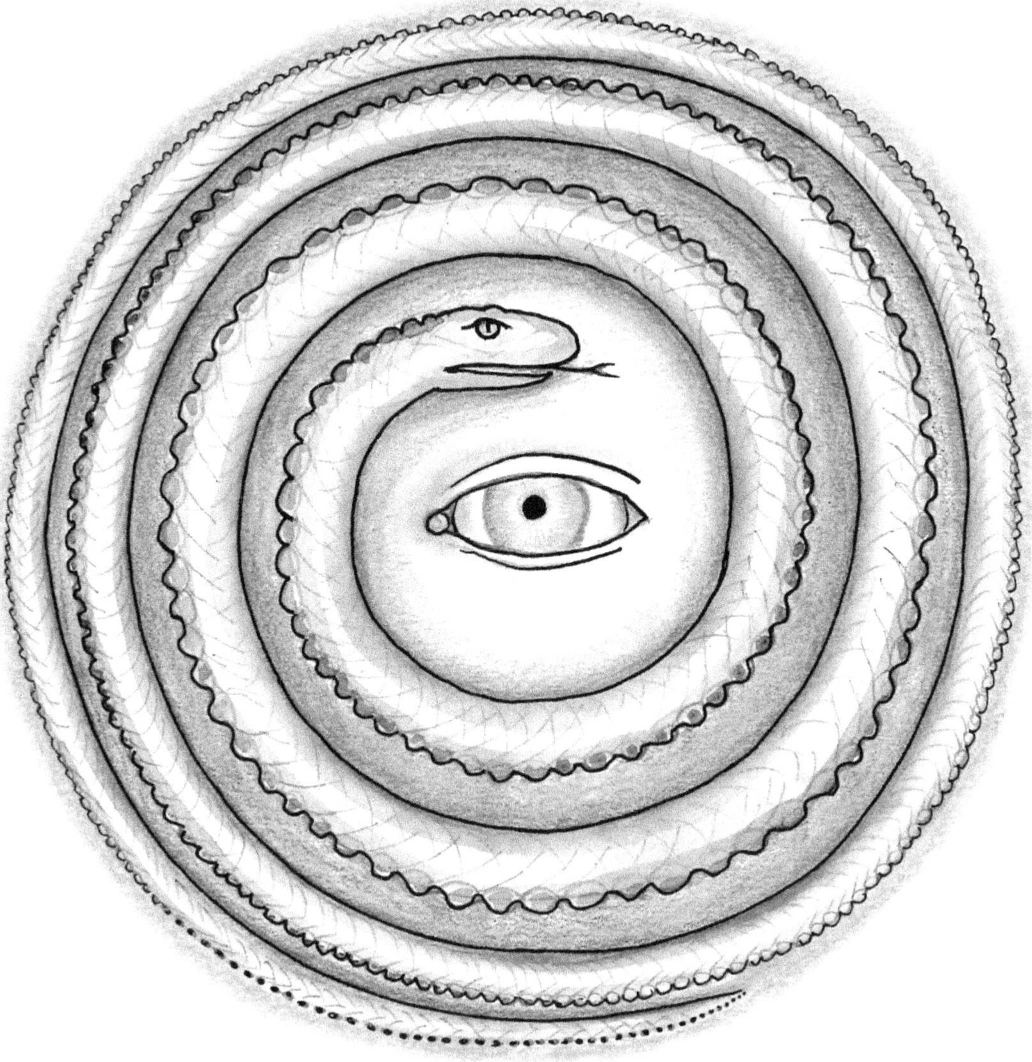

Figure 4. The emergence of human consciousness.

What a piece of work is a man! how noble in reason! how infinite in faculties! in form and moving how express and admirable! in action how like an Angel! in apprehension how like a god! the beauty of the world, the paragon of animals! And yet to me, what is this quintessence of dust?

—*Hamlet*. Act II, Scene ii, 319–323

The intelligence of our hominid ancestors developed over millions of years. The eventual emergence of human consciousness has been its spectacular and problematic result. Apart from it being impossible to be objective about itself, consciousness is both material and immaterial, matter and spirit. It will never yield its inmost secrets to purely materialist analysis.

The immediate precursors of human consciousness lie in our animal and hominid past which deeply influence our human psychology, while its full development demonstrates extraordinary features of self-awareness, aesthetics, a search for meaning, and even transcendental hunger. The development of human consciousness is the alchemy of evolution.

Since Part I deals with origins, then human *essential* nature, the origins from which we start, is the subject of this chapter. Every major philosophy and religion has its theory of human nature. Clearly, there is no definitive account of this elusive subject but a certain view of human nature naturally underpins any work such as this. It will be helpful to explain this now.

What is human nature?

Human nature is the uneasy amalgamation of five interconnected and overlapping parts of our development: animal inheritance, emotional structure, conscious ego intelligence, the unconscious, and higher consciousness. Although these evolve into one another, in some cases across millions of years, this is not a harmonious combination, but a rough unity of conflicting parts. Yet, there is also a transformational intelligence within the psyche of mankind, which is capable of creating harmony within itself, diminishing repression and domination by the malevolent side of its nature. Jung termed this the archetype of the Self.

Animal inheritance. To limit mankind's instinctual foundation to aggressive and sexual impulses (the id) is to underestimate our vast inheritance. Mankind originated from the Great Apes, which provide a reservoir of evolved genetic intelligence, ninety-six per cent of our genes, foundational not only to our body but to our consciousness (see Appendix One). The Great Apes can use and shape many types of tools; they have a capacity for empathy; they can mourn their dead and display grief; they know that their fellows possess minds; they have intense bonds between mother and child, they can be tender, have bonding rituals, and can care for each other. Chimps can share and divide food in an equal manner, they have hierarchies, leaders, and complex social dynamics. Certain chimps have been taught to count and have a keyboard vocabulary of a few hundred words; they can gamble and calculate elementary risk; they have sense of self—the list can go on, since their high level of animal intelligence is impossible to deny. Not only our instinctual inheritance, but also the foundations of our emotional intelligence and even key foundation blocks of our rational intellect (basic number and word recognition), we owe to our primate inheritance.

There are darker sides to our nature that are also developments from animal inheritance. The most obvious is our intense selfishness and our personal consumption, not just of food but of all material goods. Human beings, like the Great Apes, can be very concerned with their status and territory; they can threaten, demand submission, take the high ground, rejoice in domination and its rewards; they can engage in rape, as well as vicious and unprovoked attack. Aggressive, predatory, sexual, and killing instincts, when incorporated into the human personality, pass through the lens of ego consciousness and can become disturbed and magnified. Where an animal defends territory, humans defend countries or their identity; where one group of apes engages in unprovoked attack on another, humans subdue and enslave other nations. In addition, the elaboration and distortion of certain animal instincts and behaviour within a disturbed or traumatised human psyche is one source of what has been called vice, evil, or sin. Unconscious hatred and human malevolence are very strong—expressed both to other animals, to the earth, and even to our own species. Inter and intraspecies violence occurs in many animals but human beings are psychopathically apt at destroying their own kind. Everything concerning human beings has somehow evolved from nature.

Emotional structure. As life evolves from the simple to the complex, instincts evolve into emotion. Thus, mammals have a far more variegated emotional structure than reptiles, and as they evolve into the higher reaches of the primates, emotional structure, still rooted in instincts, achieves a great range and intensity (Bekoff, 2000). It has been widely believed up to very recently that animals do not have feelings or even that they do not physically suffer like human beings. This is very convenient, since a great number of them are butchered for our food or have been intensely worked by humans. As the primate brain expanded, eventually reaching the size and complexity of the late hominids, then a far greater and more differentiated emotional structure developed.

Ego consciousness is the combination of rational intelligence plus a distinct personality characterising developed *Homo sapiens* who emerged in East Africa *circa* 200,000 years ago (see Appendix One). Rationality, however, does not begin with modern humans. Our forebears, such as Homo habilis and erectus, who existed from around two million years ago, developed components of rational intelligence for which there is archaeological evidence (tools, weaponry, construction, use of fire). There were other species, such as Neanderthalis, who pre-existed and coexisted with *Homo sapiens* for a short period, that show care of the sick and intentional burials long before *Homo sapiens* emerged. Key components of our intelligence, awareness, and empathy clearly evolved prior to *Homo sapiens*, who inherited this expanded potential.

The ego of *Homo sapiens* evolved as a stabilising force between the great opposites of negative and positive experiences typifying mankind's early psyche, reflecting an intense and ambivalent enmeshment in nature. The larger brain had to have a master co-ordinator to allow it to function effectively, to focus and plan in order to augment the chances of the survival of individuals and the species. Ego consciousness is the integration of multiple brain functions so that a version of "reality", both subjective and objective, can exist. It co-ordinates the greatly increased frontal cortex of *Homo sapiens* and its links to the rest of the brain. It creates time, space, and causality, thus bringing our experience into conscious existence, making the outside world appear objective, giving us a sense of "reality", which is a construct of consciousness. The ego separates the individual from the world, it distinguishes "this" and "that", above and below; differentiation makes analysis and reason possible; the ego ends *participation mystique*, which is an identity or enmeshment without boundaries between mankind and nature, or child and mother. The ego is the subjective sense of identity that is the centre of personality. It implies the emergence of self-awareness in a creature, separated from the world, that can eventually examine its motives, explore its emotions, reflect upon its very thinking, and express itself in various symbolic forms, such as art and music but especially language. It co-evolves with the awareness of death and love. As self-awareness develops in early humans, they become acutely aware of death, both of their own and those they are close to. Some of the first archaeological evidence we have of *Homo sapiens* are burial practices with symbolic objects, which probably indicate the emergence of love equal to the awareness of death, an attempt to overcome death with the immortal, to transcend division and separation with a symbolic union.

The ego is also the tool for repression of parts of the psyche, such as strong emotions, so that thinking or focused concentration can take place. Mankind's ego consciousness operates seemingly by an act of will permitting mental activity to take place without being invaded by other parts of the psyche or even by the external environment. This repression, although weak at first, over time becomes a structurally in-built feature of *Homo sapiens'* mind and personality. The ego also becomes a system to protect the personality from anxiety and threat, employing an elaborate system of defences. *Homo sapiens* became the world's first repressed creature.

The ego, however, is more than just another experiment in evolution, a new mutation of genes that happen to have survival advantages. It is also a vehicle of meaning in a world which possessed no conscious expression up to this time. *Homo sapiens* is the problematic embodiment of meaning and awareness in an animal.

The ego, besides being the "subject of consciousness" is also the focal centre of personality. Again this is not unique to humans; animals also have distinct characteristics and personalities. Personality originates in the psyche-soma complex, manifesting itself at first as bodily characteristics, for example, vitality, boldness, curiosity, determination, defiance, happiness, interaction, connection, etc.—or their opposites. Personality is then shaped by social interaction, of which the most important is that with the mother and the family. Much of personality is therefore unconscious but the ego becomes its centre since personality is where the unconscious meets the world of social interaction—and the ego is the subjective centre of this also.

In the later stages of the rapid flowering of human consciousness, as *Homo sapiens* builds civilisation, the psyche undergoes a split between consciousness, centred upon ego and personality, and the unconscious, which is that part of the psyche now repressed. As civilisation develops, this repression increases. Layers of the collective unconscious underlie the platform upon which consciousness is erected through the development of civilisation by the means of political, social, and economic development. In contemporary Western capitalism, for example, the previous layers of patriarchal religions, and then nature worship, lie, like archaeological strata, underneath the top soil of civilisation.

Human nature, from a spiritual and moral perspective, contains both creative and destructive potential, the light and dark components of the psyche, the origins of which also lie in mankind's animal nature. But in animals these have no moral significance. The killing instinct of the wolf or the nurture of the animal mother for her young are part of nature and the requirements of survival. In humans this is different, for these links to our animal nature are now intensified by ego consciousness, which is central to human identity. The aggressive components of animal inheritance become distorted and magnified by negative experiences in the formation of ego identity, for example, disturbances in the womb, in perinatal or post-natal experience. Moreover, mankind's destructive potential threatens the human species and is potentially the greatest threat to all life on earth.

The unconscious is the greater part of the psyche outside of consciousness. When our human ancestors were immersed in nature there was no unconscious since self-awareness was hardly existent. Repression did not exist since they were simply part of nature. With the emergence of *Homo sapiens* the ego provided an automatic filter for consciousness which became more selective and therefore repressive of impulses, instincts, and emotions. This mechanism of selection and repression also evolved out of animals some of which also possess a similar mechanism—for example, when some animals hunt they can totally focus and ignore (i.e. repress) physiological needs (immediate hunger). The difference between animals and *Homo sapiens* is that the latter begins to do this more consciously as a result of the increasing importance of ego intelligence.

In addition, as mankind entered into civilisation then the forces of repression increased as the requirements for order, self-control, hygiene, sexual restraint, limitation of aggression, respect for others, and obedience to law or tribal rules increased. In order for large family groups and small tribes to become cohesive the *incest taboo* became stronger and more vital to the survival of the group. These repressive requirements became internalised as patriarchal religions gathered forceful grip and prohibitions became sanctioned by divinity and punishment. Repression, and therefore the unconscious, grow as civilisation advances. The unconscious is also partially created by defence mechanisms, by which consciousness defends itself against that which is painful, unacceptable, or anxiety-provoking, including components of our animal nature such as sexuality and aggression. These repressed components do not disappear, however, but are liable to erupt into consciousness, be projected on to others, or be lived out without the subject being aware of their origin. This is the *shadow* of consciousness. The discovery of the unconscious has reshaped our view of human nature. Three aspects are relevant to our argument.

A. *The psychosomatic unconscious.* The whole of the brain has a genetic and neuro-chemical base underpinning all aspects of consciousness and the unconscious. It is no longer possible to split the human neatly between body and mind. These are interconnected, for instance, the influence of dopamine and serotonin upon our consciousness and moods. Human consciousness is deeply and mysteriously interconnected with its material platform. Yet, intelligence precedes human consciousness. It coexists with the material base. The body, for instance, has a powerful healing intelligence that originates and operates outside of our consciousness.

B. *The emotional (personal) unconscious* with buried memories, complexes, or even traumas, is derived from past experience and heavily influenced by early relationships. It is the first layer of the psyche contacted by consciousness as it engages in self-exploration, typically containing personal character traits, personal history, early attachment relationships, complexes, and traumas. The personal unconscious is the route to the deeper psyche.

C. *The collective unconscious* is a foundational layer of the psyche common to all humanity. It is the deepest part of the psyche, containing both higher and lower elements, instincts and archetypes, libido and healing intelligence. It has multiple centres of healing intelligence as well as the central ordering archetype of the Self. In the depths of the unconscious there is an archetypal realm, a numinous collective unconscious beyond the personal psyche with its complexes, traumas, neuroses, and personal history. This is frequently denied and repressed by materialist civilisations. Being outside the ego, it is in a *participation mystique* with the world, an enmeshment with nature.

The higher self. There is evidence of care of the sick (and therefore potential altruism, perhaps love) in early hominids, that is, before the emergence of *Homo sapiens*. There exist 1.5 million-year-old bone fragments of a *Homo erectus* female with an advanced state of hypervitaminosis A (Walker, Zimmerman, & Leakey, 1982), which could not have been reached without considerable care. There is also evidence from the skull of a ten-year old Neanderthal child, dated at 530,000 years old, which was found to have craniosynostosis (a debilitating birth defect); the child could not have survived without care (see Appendix One). It seems, then, from archaeological evidence, that Neanderthals took care of some of their chronically ill (Spikins et al., 2010). *Homo sapiens* evolved 200,000 years ago. The first evidence we currently possess of the potential of higher consciousness, however, is intentional burial with symbolic objects around 100,000 years ago. But it is from around 40,000 years ago that we have its first decisive expression in the famous Palaeolithic cave paintings in modern day Spain and France. Higher consciousness consists of those components of the human psyche, apparently superfluous to our physical survival, that demonstrate extraordinary aspects of our psyche, such as its capacity for art, literature, and spiritual expression. It is linked to centres of the psyche that have unusual powers, such as those of illumination and intuition. The higher self is a force within human beings that compels some people to give up the dominants of their personality, put aside their ego interests, and aim for something higher, constituting a conviction that the transcendent exists and that humans can achieve it. The most frequent reason for such extraordinary efforts is an inner drive to articulate personal suffering, to overcome the fragmentation of conscious existence and undergo the eternal journey of transformation. The higher self, intensely experienced, is an ecstatic shattering of the ego and an awareness of a transpersonal reality. It leads to the conviction that the transcendent exists not only outside but also within. It relativises the ego-self, the appetites of our animal inheritance, and leads to our true centre.

Higher consciousness, in evolutionary terms, comes into existence as a reaction to the alienation experienced by the psyche as a result of the birth of the ego. Ego intelligence, individualised consciousness, and personality, break the previous wholeness of the psyche, which fragments and splits into different components, producing an alienated and repressed being. At the same time, it becomes traumatically aware of death. The Self, the inner archetype of order, pushes for the repair of this division and encourages closer contact with the higher self. It aims to replace ego aims and personality interests, the old self, with the newly emerging self, which heals the wounds of its own division. The higher self replaces or modifies the dominance of consciousness traumatised by death awareness. The archetype of the Self lies in the unconscious but, in so far as it rises into consciousness and becomes expressed and experienced, it transforms into the higher self.

At the centre of the human psyche is the Self, the central archetype of order, a directive function orchestrating the development of personality. There is an ordering principle, a natural healing intelligence, a guiding centre in the unconscious that can be contacted by many means, including dreams or simply by truly "listening to oneself". The task of the mature ego is to adapt to this inner centre. This alignment to the deep centre is necessary for the individuation process in Jungian psychology. The natural healing intelligence of the psyche is capable of repairing emotional damage and exists at all levels of the psyche—for example in meditative awareness, within the emotional or personal unconscious, and also in the deep psyche. The Hindus refer to such centres as chakras.

We do not classify the Self as a sixth component of human nature since it pervades the whole psyche from top to bottom, determining its development and growth. It arises out of a natural biological intelligence and is a natural, core, integrative intelligence, transcending individual or separate components of the psyche. The ego may think it is master in its own house but this is an illusion. Dreams, for example, are created by the Self, which constructs highly compact, richly symbolic narratives full of personal meaning that are, at first, scarcely comprehensible to ego consciousness. A crucial aspect is that they have a personal moral dimension, not of law or religion, but of psychological and spiritual growth. They are often witty, condensed, multilayered, and only truly accessible when the analytic consciousness is switched off and a looser, intuitive, symbolic, and feeling-orientated consciousness takes over. This is the psychological and spiritual growth process that guides human beings through development, conflict, and towards higher development. The world's religions, myths, and fairy tales, an enormous amount of drama, poetry, literature, music, and artistic expression are vehicles of symbolic communication for this development of the Self, the evolved essence of *Homo sapiens*.

In brief, the unconscious has multiple centres of activity, healing intelligence as well as the central ordering archetype of the Self. Our human nature is, then, a mixture of different components—animal, emotional, conscious and unconscious, as well as a higher self. The origin of human negativity may lie in creaturely selfishness but in its magnified form is the distortion of certain animal instincts and behaviour patterns as they filter through the heightened vulnerability and potentially damaged layers of human consciousness. However, at the core of human nature is a remarkable function, the Self, which is an inner director of the psyche, just as there is a bodily intelligence that from the moment of inception is director of the development process from fertilisation to full human growth. The human problem is that given its complex, combinatory nature some parts of the psyche, especially the ego, may ignore, deny, or repress this natural intelligence. Moreover, while the Self exists within human individuals it does not concretely exist for the human collective as a whole, which instead usually organises itself via law, morals, reason, or its appetites. While individuals therefore have the possibility of an inner corrective function and healing intelligence, society has no such automatic, corrective mechanism. The collective can destroy itself if it is mistaken in its reasoning, policies, or organisation. It is therefore of enormous importance that the collective creates representations of the self so that it also can find guidance.

The opposites are pushed apart,
The realms of form arise.
Consciousness emerges now,
As light and dark divide.
The sun fast rises in the sky,
The moon below descends.
With ego's birth the earth has changed,
Its unity now ends.

Figure 5. The opposites are formed.

The purpose of human consciousness

Human nature exists, then, at different levels. The first purpose of consciousness is to fulfil each of these in a balanced manner. However, the complexity of this system is an uneasy combination, and each level tends to replace and even repress lower levels. The fulfilment of our creaturely or animal existence requires the meeting of our needs for security, food, and reproduction. These factors shade into basic human emotions that deeply influence human character, for instance, early attachment which is centred on the mother–infant relationship—very similar to that of primates. Disruptions to this form disturbances in later growth, both in primates and humans. John Bowlby's theories of early attachment (Bowlby, 1969, 1973) form one of the central platforms for understanding later character and behavioural disturbance.

The fulfilment of our emotional needs is a vital part of human growth. A mature and complete human being has a wide range of emotions, aliveness, and vitality. These are especially important in engaging in relationships of intimacy and friendship. The first system of thought to view human emotionality comprehensively has been psychoanalysis, followed by a wide range of psychotherapies. Those who have suffered damage in infancy frequently have problems with their emotional structure. There exist many techniques to facilitate emotional healing, but there also exists an inner intelligence in the psyche capable of self-healing.

Ego formation is the development of a distinct individualised consciousness plus a personality formation, like a fingerprint uniquely characterising each human being. An enormous labour is invested by most parents, not only on the physical survival of their children, but in the development of this ego formation. By this means, children are given maximum chance for survival and self-development, and hopefully happiness, which often means that the ability to have relationships, and to reproduce and pass on genes, is ensured. The ego formation usually serves the needs of creaturely existence; it just employs more efficient and rational ends to achieve them. In Hume's (2007) famous aphorism, "Reason is, and ought only to be, the slave of the passions." However, the dominance of ego consciousness comes at a high cost to our sense of harmony since, while serving the long term needs of the id (our instinctual foundation) for gratification, it acts as a repressive mechanism. On the one hand, as Freud argued, this controls the id's short term and immediate demands, but on the other, the ego also represses (and filters out) higher consciousness—the world's religions consistently argue that the ego is an obstacle to spiritual growth. Although the distinguishing features of *Homo sapiens* are often claimed to be the use of reason and the development of personality, these are only part of our nature.

Psychoanalysis is also the first discipline to bring into scientific focus the existence of the unconscious. From the twentieth century onwards, under the impact of our knowledge of the unconscious, human nature must be viewed differently. The purpose of human maturation is to bring unconscious contents into consciousness—as Freud noted: "Where id was, there ego shall be". The intention of psychoanalysis is … "to strengthen the ego, to make it more independent of the super-ego, to widen its field of perception and enlarge its organization, so that it can appropriate fresh portions of the id … It is a work of culture" (Freud, 1933a).

As well as our instinctual needs, emotional requirements, and rational development, there are also components of our nature that frequently, though not in everybody, require development. These include aesthetic and purely symbolic creations that have no survival value, which are referred to here as the higher self. Although potentially existing throughout the species, this component is not like instincts, which are nearly universally experienced. The connection to, and ability to express, the higher self is not spread evenly in a human population. Nevertheless, it is particularly expressed by certain individuals who, if they do not articulate and live this part of themselves, become, as it were, spiritually crippled. This particularly applies to those who have experienced intense emotional suffering and need to find the healing energy in the higher self, especially its transcendent capacity, since normal healing intelligence in the rest of psyche is impeded.

Physical and biological evolution have an inherent movement towards greater complexity and intelligence. The emergence of consciousness in animals, and its flowering into self-consciousness and advanced intelligence in humans, is part of this evolution. There is an intelligence or spirit built-in, coexistent, and co-emergent in evolution itself. It, too, seems to have purpose and direction—human consciousness is the current stage of development of this process on earth. This consciousness is the first to be aware, not only of itself, but of the planet and its life. It is also the first to reflect back, to hold a small and misty mirror to this evolved creation.

PART II

CONSCIOUSNESS EMERGING FROM NATURE

While *Homo sapiens* evolved 200,000 years ago with a brain the size and shape of contemporary humans, it was not until around 40,000 years ago that truly modern humans emerged, as evidenced by a "great leap forward" in tools, weapons, and domestic artefacts at that time and, especially, by the astounding cave paintings discovered in Spain and France. The artistic sophistication of these creations indicates that human beings had developed an aesthetic consciousness. By 20,000 years ago the principle of an overarching life force, the Great Mother, had probably been formulated, indicating that by this time some human beings possessed a higher consciousness beyond material survival needs. Mankind had evolved from nature and was still partially immersed in it. This age of nature gods and nature worship lasted up to the patriarchal religions and civilisations that emerged around 5,000 years ago (Cashford & Baring, 1993).

The cosmic principles of creation and destruction express themselves in the opposites that lie at the foundation of human consciousness. These are experienced as the good and the bad mother, the creative and the destructive in nature and in ourselves. Consciousness developed out of this primary ambivalence, which is rooted in nature as well as our psyche, and evolved into civilisations which repressed the worship of instinct and nature.

Part II presents this foundational stage of human consciousness as a deep immersion in nature but, at the same time, the start of an emergence from it. This period of human development is presented not as a benevolent Garden of Eden but as a combination of opposites reflecting the creative and destructive forces of evolution that, later, manifest in the human psyche as good and evil. The first three chapters show the opposites of nature and the psyche in their benevolent and malevolent aspects.

Chapter Four presents the experience of nature as "The good mother".

Chapter Five, "Fertility and power", reinforces this theme with the importance of fertility worship in early humanity, a central aspect of the Great Mother.

Chapter Six, "Earth's terror" presents the opposite principle, the destructive mother, malevolent nature, the harsh struggle for existence, the necessity of aggression and killing instincts, and the awareness of death.

Chapter Seven, "The opposites at the root of consciousness", illustrates how these opposites in human nature, the destructive and creative, were viewed by early Egyptian civilisation, with an awareness, embodied in their myths, of especial interest and importance.

Chapter Eight, "The Book of Job", switches to a parallel civilisation, the Judaic. It interprets the final chapters of this extraordinary book of the Old Testament which, in the view of the author, demonstrate the lost world of the Great Mother and nature worship.

Chapter Nine, "Dragon fight", presents the violent transition from the Great Mother to patriarchal religions, encapsulated in the killing of the dragon (symbol of the Great Mother) and the establishing of a masculinised consciousness. This transition is the start of the second major movement of human consciousness.

CHAPTER FOUR

The good mother

Nature's garden, wondrous love,
pulsing through the heart.
It is our earth, it is our soul,
These two should never part.
Child with mother, earth with man,
So sweet the senses swoon.
Union born of precious love,
We must prevent its ruin.

Early mankind's experience of nature splits into the good and the terrible mother. The good mother represents the abundance and fertility of the earth as well the positive and loving ground of our psyche.

Figure 6. Earth's goodness.

The cosmic principles of creation and destruction pulse through all nature and life forms. The spectrum of mankind's early psyche reflects our experience of nature: on the one hand, of goodness and light, on the other, of darkness and death. Let us look at each in turn.

The good mother is the state of oneness experienced by the psyche, a state of harmony within itself and with nature. She represents the beneficent principle of creation, the foundation of our being. In the early period of the development of our species, the embryonic ego was a small island in the ocean of the unconscious. It was precarious, and surfaced periodically, easily and swiftly falling back into the goodness of the Great Mother, the unconscious, where it was secure and nourished. Psychologically, this state in early infancy is a foundation for health and the capacity to love; when disturbed, non-existent, or traumatised, then damage ensues; when enjoyed, a sense of confidence, happiness, and security develops. It is the psychological foundation for development.

In the early history of mankind the world was partially experienced as the good mother, loving, abundant, and fruitful, in a state of continual rebirth. The ancestors of mankind, hominids and early humans, were at first totally immersed in nature. The first paintings of human beings that we are aware of, in caves in France and Spain, starting at *circa* 40,000 years ago, show a *participation mystique*, an envelopment with nature. Her emblems of fertility and power were the dominants of our early psyche.

This original experience of oneness is subsequently forever longed for. It is the template for love and union. It is projected into all loving relationships and continually desired so as to compensate for the isolation of individualised consciousness. It is carried within us as a sense of goodness and wholeness, especially in our bodies, for example, in exercise or sexuality. It is experienced in the healing influence of nature, the beauty of sea and mountains, flowers and trees; it can be enjoyed with animals that may be our companions; it is particularly connected to the experience of love, but it can be experienced simply in ourselves as a sense of aliveness and vitality.

It is, more esoterically, the mystical core of spiritual endeavour, the experience of wholeness within the Self, the harmony of conflicting components of the psyche. In Genesis it is portrayed as a garden in which Adam and Eve, our primal archetypal selves, lived in harmony with each other, the earth, and with God, in a state of oneness without division. In every human it is the archetype of the most powerful and lasting of earthly love, that between mother and child. However, it is also achievable in the present by almost all human beings. It is our natural inheritance.

Thus, goodness, wholeness, and health can be active at all levels—physical, mental, and spiritual. Love can even be a purely inner experience without external reference—the natural wholeness of the self. It requires that the planning, worrying, and repressive aspects of ego consciousness be switched off, even if just temporarily, so that healing intelligence, the gift of nature, evolution, the Great Mother, freely available within us, can permeate our bodies, minds, and spirit.

CHAPTER FIVE

Fertility and power

Fertility is nature's child,
Around the world she runs.
No person can resist her charms,
All dancing to her drums.
Her treasure chest is open wide,
Wild spirits do descend.
Bind Odysseus to that mast
Or sure his journey ends.

Early mankind lived in participation mystique *with nature; its fertility and abundance had immense impact on our psyche. Reproductive instincts and sexuality are archetypal parts of ourselves. Nature is also overpowering. At first, human beings are small in relation to its power, but later become more powerful as they understand, manipulate, control, and destroy it.*

Figure 7. Fertility.

The creative life force manifests itself in fertility and power. The biological imperative of survival dominates all creatures, including mankind. This translates into two parts: first, personal or group survival in the present; second, species survival across time. To achieve this end, the masculine and feminine split into two respective archetypes, power and fertility, that deeply influence *Homo sapiens* even to the present. Reproductive instincts evolved into fertility rites, so evident in early civilisations but which existed long before them. Power and fertility are therefore the direct manifestation of this life force and exist in opposition to the threat of extinction. Life and death, creative and destructive forces, are intertwined in timeless embrace and constitute the framework for the history of all species including our own.

Fertility and power are archetypes in human evolution since they rise out of instincts, from our unconscious, passing through all levels of the human psyche: first, in our animal inheritance, where sexuality (fertility), dominance and aggression (power), as well as related features such as display (creativity), and submission (receptivity) play their role; second, in our hominid and early *Homo sapiens* history where increasing intelligence, manifesting in weaponry, hunting, fire, etc., provided us with more power and therefore greater fertility of our species; third, in the higher self of *Homo sapiens*, for example, in our preoccupation with art and beauty, which is the manifestation of the power of spiritual intelligence and the fertility of creative imagination.

At all these evolutionary levels of the human psyche, animal, rational, and spiritual, the life forces of fertility and power, Eros and libido, are so strong within us because we face death. At the level of the spiritual imagination, *Homo sapiens*, anguished by the awareness of inevitable extinction, reaches out for immortality, to transcend self-limitation and time. Early mankind, the creators of beauty, even left handprints on the Palaeolithic cave walls, possibly the earliest mark of individuality and spiritual consciousness on the planet. Art and beauty are our healing responses to the anguish of death.

Humankind, throughout most of its history, has been obsessed with fertility and power in their many manifestations. It is easier to see in early humanity, but contemporary fascination with wealth, consumption, sexuality, and narcissistic celebrity worship are just some examples of our endless subservience to these dominants. Prehistoric mankind, from 50,000–5000 years ago (i.e. from the emergence of fully "modern" *Homo sapiens* up to the birth of "modern" civilisations) shows the importance of these motifs in the early human psyche. The cave paintings demonstrate identification with animals, an immersion in nature: the strength of horse, fierceness of lion, power of bison; as well as nature's endless fertility. Humans were awed by the creatures of the earth, worshipping them or incorporating their spirit.

The first cave paintings from 40,000–30,000 years ago, do not display divine figures or even symbols. It is as if early humans stare out, visually entranced by the magnificence of the creatures they face. The longer one looks at these animals on the cave walls, the more one absorbs what the artist felt—their power, magnificence, beauty, and fertility. Here, one surely sees the first instinctive worship of nature. These paintings were deep in the darkness of caves, sometimes hundreds of yards from the entrance, through uterine passages back to the inner sanctum, the womb, where we see the wonderful creatures of nature. Early humans crawled, like children, back to the womb of the Great Mother to be reborn. The human mind reveals a numinous sensitivity to the essence of nature—its vitality, regenerative power, and variety. In celebrating power and fertility *Homo sapiens* rejoices in animal and natural being. Fertility worship, as this was to develop into, is the celebration of the power of nature and the awe of sexuality. It is our earliest dependency, the foundation of our love of the earth and of what was later to become the awareness and worship of the Great Mother. This layer of the collective unconscious lies at a foundational level in the human psyche. The most obvious way in which it is experienced is sexuality, where the instinctual forces of power and submission, display and creativity, entrapment and conquest, delight and consumption are the route to the most intense pleasure and orgiastic release. These forces of sexuality are hard-wired into animals and also human beings, and are deeply responsive to signalling mechanisms that release hormonal and neurotransmitter activity, flooding the animal or human body and brain, taking it over, and demanding behavioural, sexual response. The signals, according to different species, may vary. In humans and primates, visual signals are of especial importance. These include, at their most basic, visual signals of the human body and the body parts. Thus, all parts of the human body can be imbued with sexual significance, as well as those of the reproductive organs themselves. The human imagination is enormously attached to, and expands enormously, its instinctual base.

Over the next 20,000 years this immersion in fertility and power develops into the awareness that there is a principle underlying nature and her creatures. From animal and nature worship humans become aware of a general force with a power and fertility permeating all creation. At this point humans are, as it were, half in nature and half out, like a child being born. Some early figurines, dating from around 20,000 years ago, show half-human and half-animal composites. Female representations, popularly called Venuses (termed Mother Goddesses by Cashford and Baring, 1993), are very numerous and are closely focused on reproductive aspects of the body, with the head or face almost non-existent—early mankind represented itself as embedded in nature with individuality scarcely formed.

While animal worship, animism, and nature worship are early experiences of *Homo sapiens*, it is their later natural development into the cult of the Great Mother that can be discerned at the birth of the great civilisations. Thus, a female principle, and in some cases religions with prominent goddesses, can be glimpsed at the start of the patriarchies around five thousand years ago all over the Mediterranean and beyond: Nut and her daughter Isis in Egyptian mythology, Kali in Hindu mythology, Ninsun, mother goddess in Mesopotamia, Inana in Sumeria, Cybele and Rhea, Hera and Demeter, mother goddesses of Greece, and many more. These had existed for millennia prior to the emergence of civilisations, now constituting a layer of the contemporary psyche, its unconscious.

Beneath the fertility and power of nature and the psyche lies the creative, living essence itself. We approach this power by observing nature with the inner eye, with the awakened senses that, returning to their original condition, as if to a Garden of Eden, may enter into mystical communion with nature. For this to happen the ego, the repressive and filtering apparatus that enwraps the mind in the mantle of consciousness, must be suspended. As Blake commented: "If the doors of perception were cleansed everything would appear to man as it is, Infinite. For man has closed himself up, till he sees all things thro' narrow chinks of his cavern" (Blake, 1975). This opening of the doors of perception, a freeing of our vision, may be experienced as a miraculous participation in nature, the dissolving of the egoic boundaries that determine, but limit, our consciousness.

Despite all of this fertility and power of nature, the endless creation of the Great Mother, and early mankind's worship of her, there is an enigma at the heart of this experience—that of *Homo sapiens*. The fertility, power, beauty, and numinosity that we see in nature are partly a projection of the creativity of our own psyche, which is part of nature. We also are children of the Great Mother, yet we are different from all else. Mankind cannot be totally immersed in nature as soon as there is an observing eye, a separating intelligence, an ego consciousness that has differentiated sufficiently to be awed yet can observe and represent. The great early "works of art" on the Palaeolithic cave walls are at the early stages of the differentiation of the psyche out of its matrix, a consciousness which is small in relationship to the immensity of the unconscious and nature. Yet, this creature of nature, early worshipper of the Great Mother and her fertility, is destined to attack her, with profound, perhaps fatal consequences for the human species.

There once a mighty goddess lived,
she dwelt in earth and sky.
Of nature's life she is the source,
she bears us till we die.
She holds the horn of plenty,
her hand is on the womb.
All creation passes here,
as phases of the moon.

The Goddess of Laussel: a *figurine, 1.5 feet high limestone bas-relief, painted with red ochre. She holds and looks to the horn of cornucopia with thirteen notches, symbol of the phases of the moon and menstrual cycle. The absence of facial features, the hand on womb, the prominence of breasts and vulva indicate an immersion in sexuality, reproduction, and fertility while the horn points to the transpersonal nature of the Great Mother— a supremely symbolic piece,* circa *25,000 years old.*

Figure 8. The Goddess of Laussel.

CHAPTER SIX

Earth's terror

Hast thou perceived the breadth of earth?
Declare if thou dost know.
Where is the way that light doth dwell,
And how doth wisdom grow?
As for darkness, where's its home,
And when's the time for death?
Thou fear'st so much, thou can'st not know
When is thy final breath.

Adapted from Job Ch.38:
Yahweh confounds Job on his limits to the understanding of light and dark, life and death, creation and destruction.

Figure 9. Earth's terror.

Nature and Great Mother worship have, as we have just argued, a life-affirming, creative, positive quality. But there is also a darker side—that which opposes the emergence of individuality. Hence the importance of human sacrifice in these nature religions. The realm of the Great Mother demands immersion in the collective, in nature and her mysteries, in reproduction, family, and tribe. It is quite distinct from the principle of differentiation of personality and the importance of individuality that is later to develop in patriarchal religions.

Nature, besides being benevolent, is also death-threatening and appears malevolent. Survival demands aggression. Destructiveness and selfishness are vital parts of our animal, and therefore human, psyche. Our savagery is infamous. Thus, we have the opposites of nature, the good and the terrible, within ourselves. These opposites in our experience of nature, the two faces of the Great Mother, the good and the terrible, are paralleled very closely by the psychoanalytic school of Melanie Klein, which postulates (Klein, 2003) that all human infants begin life in a paranoid-schizoid state in which the good breast and the bad breast alternate as fundamental structuring experiences of the infant psyche. This duality is resolved in the "depressive position", which would find its equivalent in the history of the species as the birth of civilisation. Freud also postulated that life and civilisation emerged and developed out of two polar forces—love and hate (see Chapter Six of *Civilization and its Discontents*, Freud, 1930a).

The earth is also where all dies. It destroys all it creates. It is in constant change and life is limited, precarious, and sometimes terrifying. The earth passes from the good to the terrible mother and can be malevolent, dangerous, and wrathful. All creatures must feed on other life forms. Pain alternates with pleasure. Death and life are interdependent.

The evolution of the earth over 4.6 billion years has been a process of creative destruction. Of this immense period of time the major part (3.6 billion years) has been without multi-cellular life forms, since early conditions on the planet were inimical to life, and subsequently it took billions of years for complex cell structures to build up. Once life was established, numerous mass extinctions occurred (see Appendix Two). Life was precarious not only for individuals but for the human species. The emergence of self-reflective consciousness is strongly disposed to arise, seeded as it were into evolution, but there are many forces pitched against it. Indeed, the chief carrier of this consciousness, *Homo sapiens*, had only a slender foothold on the planet for the first 150,000 years of a precarious existence.

The psyche of hominids, our family group as we evolved from ape to human, developed over millions of years and reflected the conditions of nature. As well as goodness, mankind, a rather helpless animal without effective weapons, experienced fear and terror. We were subject to disease, early death, accident, infections; prey to reptiles, rodents, wild animals; at the mercy of volcanoes, earthquakes, floods, climate, and ecological changes. It is difficult for contemporary humans to imagine just how prolific were the life forms on the planet in our early history and how many were hostile to our existence. Nature is volatile and the life it supports is precarious. Ninety-eight per cent of earth's documented species are extinct; mankind as a species, from the beginning, lived on the edge of survival.

Despite the enormous advantages of higher intelligence, *Homo sapiens* was almost wiped out, probably just before leaving Africa (70,000 years ago) and colonising the world. It is estimated that there is more genetic diversity in a troupe of chimps than in the eight billion members of the human race. This implies a genetic bottleneck, a great reduction in human numbers at around

70,000 years ago, when the race was reduced to a few thousand individuals. Genetic evidence suggests that contemporary humans descend from a small population of 1,000 to 10,000 breeding pairs existing about 70,000 years ago (Ambrose, 1998). The most probable explanation for this was dramatic climate change caused by the dense volcanic ash from the eruption of Mount Tobo that altered the climate of Africa and probably propelled the migrations of *Homo sapiens* out of that continent. Mount Tobo (Indonesia) erupted *circa* 70,000 years ago and was 100 times more violent than any volcano in recent history. It was the "most recent super-eruption and plunged Earth into six years of volcanic winter, possibly causing a bottleneck in human evolution and significant changes to regional topography" (Savino & Jones, 2007, p. 140).

The human species, the bearer of higher consciousness, almost became extinct. Higher levels of order in evolution have to contend with enormous destructive forces in nature. Symbolically, the prolific good mother battles with the terrible and destructive. The immense forces of evolution and nature contend with disease, death, the ecological conditions of the earth, and even meteorites. Higher consciousness is not inevitable, it even requires luck.

These destructive powers of nature are augmented by the dark forces inside man's own psyche: fears and terrors, irrational outbursts, psychic epidemics, bouts of lust, murderous impulses, invasions from the unconscious, inherent instability, and disintegrations of a fragile ego under great pressure from attack, stress, anxiety, and terror. *Participation mystique*, the immersion in the unconscious and nature, is not simply beneficent, since nature and the unconscious are inherently ambivalent. The psyche of mankind can be savage, terrifying, destructive, malicious, and murderous—anti-life forces can overwhelm it. Just as the psychoanalyst Melanie Klein characterised the early psyche of the infant as a paranoid-schizoid condition, so too the early psyche of mankind was assailed by extremes before the ego emerged to abate and modify the opposites.

Human selfishness rapidly turns to greed, since the psyche experiences emptiness as a result of the repression that stems from the ego. We feel depleted or threatened and attempt to overcome our feeling of alienation by filling ourselves with material goods. More than any other animal the human brain, with its greatly expanded consciousness and sensitivity, is open to formation in early infancy, which implies it is more susceptible to emotional damage. In the birth process there are experiences deeply formative for the psyche. Grof (1985) outlines the stages of perinatal experience and their enormous impact on the emerging human being and later on in its life. Human beings also have complex defence mechanisms that attempt to defend the self or the embryonic ego from anxiety and disturbance. The inner world of the disturbed infant is therefore of a radical, severe nature and liable to trauma. Kalsched (1996) gives a powerful account of the impact of trauma on the infant psyche. Indeed, when whole cultures are subject to profound anxiety and trauma there are grounds for mass psychosis. Hitler and Germany are, of course, outstanding instances of this but there are many other examples in history.

Life itself and the human species have evolved in spite of, and sometimes because of, all these forces against it. But now it is different. The darkest force on the planet is mankind itself, who threatens the life of all species, even its own. The roots of this lie in a selfishness and destructiveness allied with a Promethean technology capable of serving narrow economic and military ends. The human psyche, spectacular though it may be, is deeply flawed as it faces its biggest challenge—preservation of the species and its planetary home.

CHAPTER SEVEN

The opposites at the root of consciousness

He lifts the light of consciousness,
Above chaotic waters.
Scarab shall our tutor be,
For lessons she has taught us.
She rolls the ball with eggs of life,
Embalmed in the mud,
Life's renewal ever mixed
With darkness and with good.

Nun, god of the waters of chaos, lifts the barque of the sun god Ra,
represented by the scarab and the sun disk,
into the sky at the beginning of time.

—*The Book of the Dead of Anhai*, circa 1050 BC

Figure 10. The light of consciousness.

The opposites of order versus chaos and creation versus destruction were central to Egyptian mythology, at the root of the gods' struggles, mankind's existence, and consciousness itself—civilisation is the temporary resolution of this conflict.

Within the psyche of early man the two great principles of creation versus destruction express themselves in the derived polarity of order versus chaos. This is expressed in the religions and myths of early civilisations, a period in which we see the worship of the Great Mother before it was replaced by the patriarchy. These opposites can be traced as structuring principles of the cosmos, evolution, life, species existence, and civilisation. They can be found at all later levels in the human psyche and underlie mankind's own creative and destructive nature, sometimes termed good and evil.

Creation myths locate the origins of human nature in the transpersonal realm rather than in mankind's own psyche. This is because up to the recent past (the Enlightenment) mankind chiefly thought mythologically and theologically about such matters as human nature, good and evil, the origins of consciousness, and so on. The symbolic truth of creation myths, however, is that they are the expressions of the birth of consciousness rather than accounts of the origins of the world—despite the intentions of the authors. Mankind possessed no theory of evolution up to very recently and therefore did not believe that human nature evolved from animals. The Hindu scriptures do, however, have references to a type of evolution and did conceive the age of the earth in billions of years—a remarkable intuition. Although this knowledge was, then, largely unavailable to the Ancients, the myths and narratives of early civilisations contain deep meta-psychological truth in symbolic form. The Chinese, Hindus, and Egyptians had a vision of the opposites that underlie mankind's struggle and posited them as universal principles—as this narrative does.

The Chinese opposites of yin (the supple) and yang (the strong) symbolise interconnected forces that underpin the universe, the human body and mind. All further opposites, male and female, darkness and light, hot and cold, water and fire, earth and air are its developments. Far from being antagonistic opposites, they are an interconnected dynamic whole and form the ancient Chinese basis for understanding the world and human nature.

Less well-known is that the ancient Egyptians held the dual principles of creation versus destruction and their corollary, order versus chaos, as being of equal importance in their mythology. Judaic civilisation is heavily influenced by the Egyptian. The sun-god, the symbol of consciousness itself, is raised by superhuman effort out of the waters of chaos, that is, out of the unconscious. Thus, the constructive creative principle, *Maat*, is the basis of civilisation, which struggles with the destructive forces against it, not only from nature, but from the darkness and violence within mankind. The scarab or dung beetle was venerated by the ancient Egyptians. It puts its eggs in dung and rolls it to a hole in the ground, where they are later to hatch. The image of the beetle rolling the ball was likened to the sun-god rolling the sun. The earth became the underworld, the nightly journey of the sun-god, and the new life from under the earth was the rising sun. Such images—life out of dung and consciousness out of dross—prefigure similar alchemical themes of the transformation of lead into gold. The connection to the life principle of sun, light, higher consciousness, and our transcendent being is necessary to combat the darkness within ourselves.

By 5,000 years ago the Neolithic revolution in agriculture had produced large, concentrated human populations, especially along subtropical river basins. Order now meant the establishment of society, law, and regulation requiring clear and firm leadership and control. Order and civilisation were synonymous. Evidently it needed not only reason to establish it, but higher forces to give it sufficient authority—the Pharaohs were divine.

The Egyptian conception of time was at two levels: first, that of the gods, in linear time consisting of narratives concerning their struggles, which constituted the archetypal principles that governed human existence and consciousness. Second, the time of mankind, which was circular, where as a result of the gods' struggles, the cycle of our existence, its daily round, was created. This cycle was not meant to last forever but, like the finale to Wagner's opera, *The Ring of the Nibelung*, one day ends, and conditions return to their beginning in the primal ocean of the unconscious. Thus, one of the earliest and long-lasting civilisations intuited not only the origins of mankind but also its possible end.

Such a battle between opposites is of both collective and personal significance and is dramatically represented by the sun itself on its daily and nightly cycles. Ra, the sun god of consciousness, rules the day but each night is devoured by the forces of darkness. Ra's reign is not secure, for each night he crosses on a barque over the waters, fights with the serpent of chaos, Apep, and requires the help of Osiris, the principle of rebirth and renewal, so as to emerge the next day. This battle between the forces of light and darkness symbolises the inner state of mankind, the nature of his psyche. The forces of order, the creative principles that have fashioned the existence of not only life but the human psyche, are threatened by chaos and destructiveness.

Figure 11. The night journey.

The sun sets dark beyond the Nile, the light of day grows dim,
And from the shadows of the mind, fear grips the soul within.
O, row your barque through gloom of night,
Death's dark and dangerous gates,
The sun god dies to be reborn, a glorious morn awaits.

Ra, the creator sun god on his night journey to do battle with the serpent of chaos, Apep.

The negative forces within our species mirror our creative potential because human consciousness is a magnified arena in which opposites can be acted out. What, in an animal, is bonding or aggression may, in humans, be love or hatred; what, in an animal, is a predatory instinct may, in humans, be intense brutality or psychopathy. The human being, considerably more complicated than any animal, has so much more that can go wrong in character formation. Human beings, from the start of life, especially in the womb and in birth experience, are extremely vulnerable, both physically and emotionally. Due to its early sensitivity the psyche easily suffers intense insecurity with serious later consequence. Some of the recent, twentieth century examples of collective psychopathic brutality, such as Nazism, show such dark negativity in our species that despair in our collective future seems an obvious conclusion. However, Egyptian mythology indicates that a battle between the light and dark sides of our nature has been part of human experience since the beginning and that the forces of rebirth may prevail.

CHAPTER EIGHT

The Book of Job

Where was't thou at foundation's birth?
Declare, if thou dost know.
Who laid earth's corner stone thereof,
Who made the heat and snow?
Can'st thou ride the north wind sharp,
Or calm the wild bull's pride?
Or can'st create the light and dark,
Or stem the ocean's tide?
Whose hand was it that formed the earth,
When morning stars did sing?
And sons of God cried out for joy,
Such glory did it bring?

Adapted from Job 38
Yahweh reveals to Job the nature of the world before his consciousness.

This famous biblical story represents the ambivalence of the shift in consciousness from nature religions and the realm of the Great Mother to patriarchal religious domination. Yahweh reveals his dark and "feminine" side as a nature god that precedes the transcendent god of law and morality.

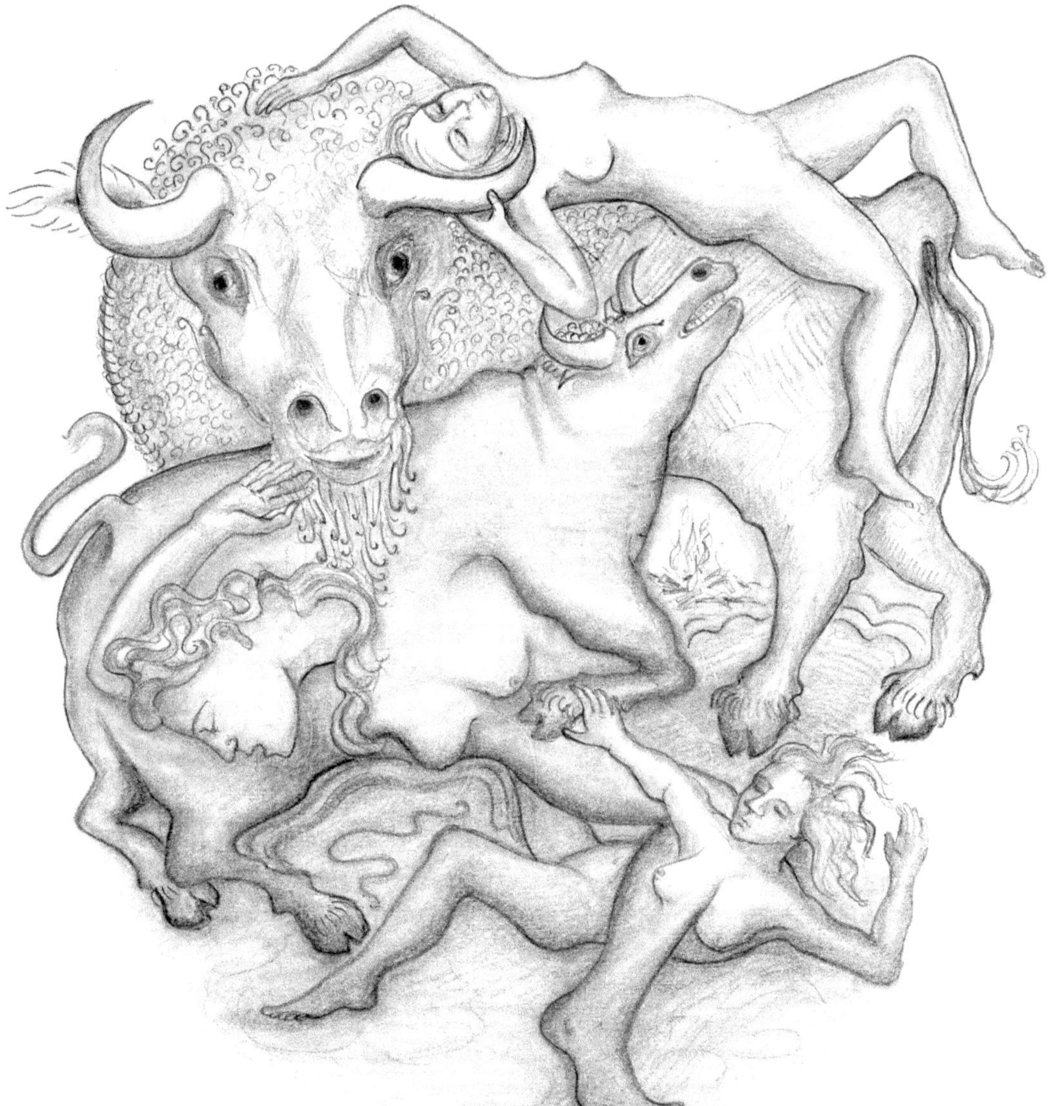

Figure 12. Fertility and power.

The Abrahamic religions, Judaism, Christianity, and Islam, stemming from a single source, had a decisive influence on human consciousness. They constituted a religious concentration on one God, transcendent to creation, whose word was embodied in law, the focus of which was overwhelmingly moral—good and evil were split into two radically different camps. It was a revolutionary transformation of consciousness that gripped the religious imagination of significant parts of the human race from the second millennium BCE. This law was intended to embrace individuals and their rulers; its vision gave meaning to mankind's relation to the cosmos, its creator, to this life, and the hereafter. So powerful was this new paradigm that it also later formed the religious and ideological basis for the development of Europe in the Middle Ages and for the Islamic world after the seventh century AD. Its foundations lay in Judaism. It constituted a shift to patriarchal religious consciousness, since it was a break from the nature religions, the spiritual and religious way of thinking and behaving that had dominated mankind for millennia, in which fertility, magic, power, spirit world, sexuality, sacrifice, superstition, and shamanistic healing were dominant.

The idea that there could be *one* prior to everything, the source of all existence, a single principle underlying the cosmos and human nature was, and is, utterly compelling. That this translated into the word of God and revealed itself through a people, prophets, gurus, or enlightened individuals was an irresistible transformative principle. The creation of whole peoples with a religious, even obsessive conscience, a superego, was a new development in human culture. In addition, such ideas of the patriarchal religious were instrumental in welding together cohesive societies and civilisations in contrast to the anarchy and barbarism that preceded and surrounded them. A reading of the early books of the Hebrew bible such as Leviticus, show a distancing of the Jewish people from their neighbours, for example, the Canaanites and the Egyptians. These ideas do not have the same force today, at least in the Western world, since they have run their course through thousands of years of religious and cultural change. Yet, they constituted a revolutionary development of human consciousness and have been motors of history.

The Book of Job, written somewhere between 1500–1000 BCE, is a pivotal drama concerning a transition in human consciousness. As well as being integral to the Jewish tradition, this tale is also told in the Koran and has entered into Christian consciousness as a compelling story of the Old Testament. Here we are concerned with one part of this intriguing tale—the problematic transition from the worship of the Great Mother to that of the patriarchal religions.

The tale can be told simply. Job is a God-fearing man who has completely obeyed Judaic law. God tests him by taking away his health, wealth, and family—pillars that supported his sense of identity. Job falls into misery and suffering but does not curse his God, remaining his true servant. Although the Judaic religion believed misfortune was the result of sin, the righteous Job does not admit such errors. He calls on Yahweh for justice, challenging him to be consistent with his revealed word. Eventually, Yahweh reveals a vision of creation that transforms Job, and that which he lost is restored. The patience of Job is rewarded; his suffering is overcome; loyalty has its final rewards.

There is no doubt that this tale has stirred the imagination of countless people across thousands of years: Job's resilience in the face of intense suffering; his loyalty to the true God in the face of apparent betrayal; his refusal to curse his fate and reject the God who has delivered him to it; the extreme loss of health, family, possessions; his restoration to wholeness as a transformed human being.

However, there is another viewpoint from which the Book of Job is not a morality drama but, instead, is at variance with the evolving orthodoxy of Judaism. It is part of *wisdom literature*, combining a Hebrew emphasis on practical wisdom with an Hellenic/Platonic concept of transcendent wisdom. (Wisdom literature in the bible refers to such books as Job, Psalms, Proverbs, Ecclesiastes, Song of Songs, the Wisdom of Solomon). The Book of Job is, really, an heretical text strangely escaping censure and becoming part of the mainstream Old Testament. This is a result of its beauty, its disguise, and its layers of profound meaning. Its beauty is of such power that it dismantles normal language and consciousness, breaking through to an archetypal level of reality—the unconscious; its disguise is of a moral tale of trial and redemption underneath which are different levels, including those of individual, mystical transformation through suffering as well as a meditation on the nature of our collective consciousness. This latter, esoteric theme is the focus of these pages.

The Jewish faith developed out of, and then in opposition to, the fertility religions of its neighbours, which continually tempted the chosen people. These religions and cults were immersed in the worship of reproduction, fertility, and the power of nature. The patriarchal religions of Islam, Judaism, and later Christianity opposed this nature worship, demanding subjection to one transcendent and moral God. This is a battle of opposites. Job represents Jewish orthodoxy, but in this tale, Yahweh, instead of rewarding Job's loyalty to the faith he had demanded, completely reverses his traditional position and presents himself as a nature god—exactly what the Jews had been fighting against.

Of the many unusual features of the Book of Job, two stand out for our thesis. First, Satan, or the *adversary*, had access to the court of Yahweh. Judaism, and indeed Christianity, were built upon the separation of good and evil. There is a tradition in Judaism of Satan, or Lucifer, being cast out of heaven for his sin of pride (Isaiah 14:4–17; Ezekiel 28; Dead Sea Scrolls) and in the Christian New Testament (Revelation 12) of Satan being identified with the dragon who is cast out in the War of Heaven only to return in the last days of the apocalypse.

> Now war arose in heaven, Michael and his angels fighting against the dragon. And the dragon and his angels fought back, but he was defeated and there was no longer any place for them in heaven. And the great dragon was thrown down, that ancient serpent, who is called the devil and Satan, the deceiver of the whole world—he was thrown down to the earth, and his angels were thrown down with him.
>
> (Revelation 12:7–9)

Although this extract is from the Book of Revelation, and therefore refers to "last days", it coincides closely with the underground literature in the Jewish and later Gnostic tradition (e.g., the Dead Sea Scrolls) which tells of a war in heaven between the forces of light and darkness before the beginning of time.

In the Book of Job there is a close relationship of Yahweh with Satan. It is Satan, which we may interpret as the darker side of Yahweh, who proposes the trials of Job. By implication,

Yahweh is not a single and united God but a union of opposites. The great dragon is also the disguise for the great mother, conceived by the religions of the patriarchy as their mortal enemy.

Second, the revelation of Yahweh is, surprisingly, of a creation that bears no resemblance to the revelation of the book of Genesis. Yahweh reveals a mysterious universe in which, not humans, but animals, such as behemoth and leviathan, are its glory. Even in translation this is one of the most extraordinary and beautiful mystical texts ever written. It is not possible to write at this level without having, in a deep manner, experienced the essence of this revelation. The words sing their vision. The Book of Job was a mystical revelation that crashed through the evolving one-sided orthodoxy of Judaism, revealing another side to the Godhead that symbolises the supreme values of human consciousness.

The revelation of Yahweh to Job can be divided into three parts.

1. Chapters 38 and 39: Yahweh confounds and overpowers Job, dismantling his consciousness with a vision of nature, the power of himself, the nature god, and the insignificance of mankind.

> By what way is the light parted, which scattereth the east wind upon the earth? ....
> Out of whose womb came the ice? and the hoary frost of heaven, who hath gendered it? ...
> Canst thou bind the sweet influences of Pleiades, or loose the bands of Orion? ....
> Canst thou send lightnings, that they may go, and say unto thee, Here we are? ...
> Who hath put wisdom in the inward parts? or who hath given understanding to the heart?
>
> (Book of Job. 38:24–31)

This is followed by a celebration of the instincts of animals and, re-emphasised, the insignificance of man in this creation.

> Wilt thou hunt the prey for the lion? or fill the appetite of the young lions ...
> Who provideth for the raven his food? when his young ones cry unto God, they wander for lack of meat ...
> Doth the hawk fly by thy wisdom, and stretch her wings toward the south?
> Doth the eagle mount up at thy command, and make her nest on high?
> She dwelleth and abideth on the rock, upon the crag of the rock, and the strong place.
> From thence she seeketh the prey, and her eyes behold afar off.
> Her young ones also suck up blood: and where the slain are, there is she.
>
> (Book of Job. 38:39–41; 39:26–30)

Yahweh reveals himself as a nature god and exposes Job's ignorance of its mysteries, as if he were saying that Job, and therefore Judaic orthodoxy, is ignorant of the real nature of creation. By means of a series of extraordinary questions Judaic consciousness is broken down, ecstatically shattered, and a new level of reality emerges in which the divinity and its mysterious paradoxical creation are one. Human consciousness dissolves its egoic illusion in order to merge with a wild and savage divine reality permeating all nature. Yahweh reveals the realm of nature, and therefore by implication the Great Mother, underlying the patriarchal religious consciousness. It is as if Yahweh becomes the Great Mother, rejoicing in the mysteries and awesomeness of nature.

2. Chapter 40: Yahweh thunders against Job for challenging him and Job ceases his protest.

> Moreover the Lord answered Job, and said, Shall he that contendeth with the Almighty instruct him? he that reproveth God, let him answer it.
> Then Job answered the Lord, and said, Behold, I am vile; what shall I answer thee? I will lay mine hand upon my mouth.
>
> (Book of Job. 40:1–4)

Thus, Job's highly righteous and defended position is broken down by the revelation of the nature god. The submission of his consciousness, its complete surrender, will lead to a mystical revelation of the repressed side of Judaism. The fertility cults are not mere pagan worship and licentious living but symbolically represent the underlying mysteries of nature and our consciousness. When the highly differentiated rational consciousness is broken one is left with a symbolic and "promiscuous" reality. At first all things flow into one another, traditional morality dissolves, normal perception alters, conventional judgements fade, repressed feeling arise. But then a transformation happens. That which was once sinful appears no longer evil; that which appeared primitive and savage now has the deeper wisdom of nature and the unconscious; that which appeared meaningless takes the form of a deeper reality. The dominants of our consciousness, its ego and superego formation, surrender their power and an underlying wholeness begins to emerge.

3. Chapter 40 and Chapter 41: the revealing of behemoth and leviathan.

Yahweh talks to Job not of law but of the original state that underlies consciousness. Job is reassured of the absolute ignorance of his tight reasoning. In answer to Job's appeal for justice the implied answer is thunderous. There is no justice. The origins of this world, this consciousness, lie in a totality of ambivalence in which life and death, power and love, leviathan and the lamb are all an original creation, before patriarchal consciousness split them into opposites. How can God cause suffering? How can he punish the righteous Job? Should not the chosen people, or the righteous, be rewarded for their good life? There is no answer from Yahweh on these questions since he is beyond any appeal and, more importantly, beyond the conscious logic of mankind, whose suffering is of no importance. Yahweh reveals another world, that preceding and underlying the patriarchy—the unconscious, the realm of the Great Mother.

Far from man being the purpose of creation, Yahweh rejoices in behemoth:

> Behold now behemoth, which I made with thee; he eateth grass as an ox.
> Lo now, his strength is in his loins, and his force is in the navel of his belly …
> He is the chief of the ways of God …
>
> (Book of Job. 40:15–16;19)

And also leviathan:

> None is so fierce that dare stir him up: who then is able to stand before me? …
> I will not conceal his parts, nor his power, nor his comely proportion …
> Out of his mouth go burning lamps, and sparks of fire leap out.
> Out of his nostrils goeth smoke, as out of a seething pot or caldron.
> His breath kindleth coals, and a flame goeth out of his mouth.
> In his neck remaineth strength, and sorrow is turned into joy before him …
> Upon earth there is not his like, who is made without fear.
> He beholdeth all high things: he is a king over all the children of pride.
>
> (Book of Job. 41:10–34)

Leviathan and behemoth are great dragon symbols of the pre-patriarchal civilisations. They are his pride. What Yahweh reveals is the religious consciousness preceding and underlying patriarchal religions. He reveals the unconscious as it was once experienced by mankind. One could be staring at the animals on the Palaeolithic cave walls. The fertility religions that Judaism repressed belonged to the oldest religious tradition on earth—that of the Great Mother.

There now follows Job's repentance and acceptance of Yahweh's revelation, culminating in his transformation. The Book of Job, from this viewpoint, is a confession-revelation. By implication, the religious patriarchal form is only a stage of man's consciousness, only a partial view. It tries to repress one side of the opposites of the creative-destructive paradox. It is incomplete and, moreover, inadequate in front of elemental nature.

An intriguing commentary on this story is Carl Jung's *Answer to Job* (1973), which, among other things, puts emphasis on the challenge provoked in Yahweh by the confrontation with Job. Jung argues that this leads ultimately to God's incarnation through Christ into man—that is, a clarification of the ambivalence in Yahweh. However, Jung also referred to the fourth, feminine aspect of God, suggesting that the Christian doctrine of the Trinity is incomplete, since it lacked this feminine dimension. The same viewpoint is also evident in the illustrations of the Book of Job by William Blake in which he brings Job's wife into the picture. One of the final illustrations of this series is of "Job and His Daughters" which conveys the same message: Job's revelation is of the feminine component of creation.

From our viewpoint, rather than presaging the future, the Book of Job reveals both the past and that which underlies one-sided Judaic and Christian orthodoxy. It reveals the realm of nature and the Great Mother, the repressed feminine side of the Godhead, immersed in reproduction, fertility, and sexuality that became associated with evil. Thus, in the patriarchal religions, man's feminine side is linked to sin. Yet here this feminine side is a deep truth.

The Book of Job therefore represents the ambivalence of the transition from one form of consciousness, nature religions and the Great Mother, to patriarchal consciousness. It is the development of the psyche on a knife point, demonstrating the difficulty and battle, the oscillation between two types of consciousness. The decisive move, in the form of the Abrahamic religions, was, however, towards a masculinised, patriarchal consciousness, and for this the killing of the dragon was the route taken by the descendants of the Abrahamic tradition. The Book of Job is therefore an anachronism, out of keeping with the general flow of Judaic history. It reveals so much because it is the counter-culture underlying the orthodoxy. Collectively it represents the repressed unconscious, the world of the Great Mother.

Leviathan, our pride and joy,
He swallows worlds entire.
He cares not for your principles,
He's made of earth and fire.
Through shadows of the universe,
He ranges 'cross the skies.
He reigned here long before the rest,
And be here when they die.

Figure 13. Leviathan.

CHAPTER NINE

Dragon fight

The hero struggles with his fate,
He rises with the sun.
He cannot rest until he's freed,
And awesome deeds are done.
The hero comes from other worlds,
His arrows are sharp-feathered.
To kill the mother of all life,
And from himself be severed.

Figure 14. Dragon fight.

Three to six thousand years ago patriarchal religions replaced Great Mother worship. The masculine became opposed to nature, the realm of the feminine, mythologically portrayed in the dragon fight. This is a fundamental shift in human consciousness and prerequisite to the advancement of patriarchal civilisation.

The story of *Homo sapiens*, so far presented, is that of an emergent consciousness founded upon a vast heritage—now the unconscious of our species. The Great Mother, in her beneficent and terrible aspects, presided over our pre-history and therefore, like a mother with child in womb or at breast, is the mythological foundation of our evolving consciousness and of the archaic roots of our unconscious. The contemporary human being has a consciousness centred in the ego, plus an unconscious, which is more than the id of sexual and aggressive forces; it is a vast inner world, quite different from our consciousness, and has its own purpose, meaning, and vibrant numinosity. It is immersed in fertility and power and founded on an archetypal, transpersonal, awesome realm with its own beauty and emotional narrative. So, also, in the history of the evolving consciousness of our species, there is a duality—the patriarchal civilisations arose by repressing the matriarchal feminine, for example, the God of the Jews forbade the worship of the cow of fertility. The consciousness of modern man is built on this repression.

Where the immersion in nature meets the numinous in our psyche lies the Great Mother, the ruling dominant of *Homo sapiens*' consciousness up to the dawn of modern civilisation and opposed to individuality. She represented collective values of tribe, custom, nature, immersed in power and fertility, close to the animal kingdom. The emergent consciousness, symbolised as masculine, is individualised. The mythological birth of the hero is the bearer of this consciousness. His parentage, secret or otherwise, is of the sky gods. His destiny is to create civilisation and therefore he deals a mortal blow to the Great Mother, he feels compelled to defeat wild animals and monsters, to decapitate the gorgon, and vanquish the dragon. The emerging individualised consciousness feels trapped in the realm of the Great Mother and its impersonal, collective, animal nature.

The killing of the dragon is an archetypal mythologem of transpersonal significance, telling a story of the consciousness of our species and how it developed. It symbolises the birth of a stage of consciousness, when it became "masculinised", individualised and differentiated from the Great Mother and its immersion in nature. Like a dream it tells it in dramatic form. The dragon is frequently portrayed as hideous—though not in our illustration since she really represents the Great Mother; the masculine consciousness is determined to kill her; the fight is brutal and violent; the hero is victorious and he carries his prize, the captive female, who is enchanted by his power and ready to be his wife, to join his household and submit to his reign in a new world. From this point on, consciousness will be different. Man, woman, all creatures, and even the earth will be different.

However, one thing has not changed. *Homo sapiens* carries the past in the depths of the psyche. Thus, under the patriarchy, the dominant civilisations for the last five thousand years, he has been a divided being and repressed his past, the foundational self—the Great Mother within. This transpersonal, archetypal event has immense importance in the development of our species since *Homo sapiens'* creative and destructive powers are without precedent. Consciousness could now soar, no longer held captive in nature's embrace. Like Icarus, mankind constructs wings to escape confinement. He may disdain his roots and think himself free of his lower nature; he may even boast to have destroyed the dragon. However, he knows not the high price to be paid since the dragon is not destroyed but is immortal and lives on—in the unconscious.

PART III

SEPARATION: THE RISE AND FALL OF CONSCIOUSNESS

The creative-destructive paradox at the centre of material evolution is foundational to the psyche of mankind. It is expressed in our ego and its separated or fallen state where extreme conflicts and divisions in our nature reach consciousness and are magnified by it. In Hindu philosophy Shakti is considered to be the creative-destructive force underlying the phenomenal universe.

Human consciousness emerged from nature worship into the world of patriarchal religions and civilisations. This happened over thousands of years but probably started around the time of the agricultural revolution (*circa* 10–12,000 years ago) when crop production and farming became possible, allowing larger concentrations of population to develop. From 5000 years ago onwards there were developments of writing, strong city development, and patriarchal religions. Certain civilisations such as the Egyptian, Canaanite, and Cretan show the marked influence of female goddesses, indicating a different relationship to the feminine. Thus, female and male divinities were simultaneously worshipped in a transition period, but by its end we observe the definite movement towards patriarchal religions as major forces in history. This was a fundamental development of human consciousness. Part III examines this transition and its consequences.

Chapter Ten, "The emergence of civilisation", begins with the dragon (Great Mother, nature worship) now defeated and the establishment of a new system of civilisation and its corresponding consciousness. While this was a necessary development of control and freedom from nature, the cost was a fundamental repression in the psyche. The history of mankind's relationship to the bull parallels the myths of the killing of the dragon and is presented as a detailed example of this transition.

The remaining chapters of Part III track the consequences of the above in one of the formative patriarchal religions, the Judaic, which massively influenced subsequent history in the Near

East and the West. Islamic and Christian religions have their roots in Judaism and the Hebrew bible.

Chapter Eleven, "The Garden of Eden", examines the most famous myth of the Hebrew Bible, an original paradise where human beings lived in harmony with nature and God. But in the Judaic religion this is a lost paradise to which we long to return. Here, this myth is treated symbolically at different levels, for example, as a primal unity in the unconscious, as well as the collective feeling of a loss in the patriarchal religions—interpreted here as the lost unity with nature and the Great Mother.

Chapter Twelve. "Lucifer" (the bringer of light) is an indispensable part of the creation story and represents the impulse to consciousness, which simultaneously is the experience of separation, alienation, and death. Later, in Christian mythology, Lucifer is conflated with Satan.

Chapter Thirteen, "Banishment", speaks of an original state of harmony, but the tasting of the fruit of the Tree of Knowledge, the birth of consciousness, is characterised as an act of disobedience. The consequence of this is "death". Consciousness breaks from the primal unconscious, a state of union, and is inevitably propelled into death awareness, a state of separation and alienation. Banishment from the Garden into a world of time, finitude, labour, and anxiety is the tragic result. Trauma is at the birth of consciousness.

CHAPTER TEN

The emergence of civilisation

He gazes at the far off town,
It rises to the skies.
The dragon gasps its dying breath,
To earth it sinks and dies.
At what cost is this destruction
What the price of lofty deed?
Urban life and civilization,
By this blood from Nature's freed.

Order now is raised from chaos,
Sexuality controlled,
Discipline will be the watchword,
Boundaries will be patrolled.
Consciousness demands such rigour,
Clear division is its goal,
You and I are separate beings,
Nature no more holds the soul.

Thoughts to new heights now do rise,
Technique shall have no bound.
Carnal impulse is contained,
Spirit touches not the ground.
Instinctual world now is repressed,
Nature's power is therefore dimmed.
In spite of freedom yet we feel
By this action we have sinned.

Great Mother into shadow fades,
Father gods shall now shine bright.
Moon descends below horizon
Sun ascends to zenith's height.

Figure 15. Emergence of civilisation.
The ascendant patriarchal, solar consciousness, in the form of the Hero, triumphs over the Great Mother, symbolised by the dragon.

The great religions and patriarchal civilisations suppressed attachments to the gods of nature, the Great Mother, and the worship of fertility and sexuality. Civilisation, requiring order, control, and an individualised, moralistic consciousness, was built on this repression.

It is customary to tell the history of mankind, including that of the emergence of civilisation, with reference to the objects or productions of consciousness—the developments in technology, the emergence of writing, the creation of surplus, new class structures, trading relationships, and so forth. Of course, these are of great importance and as well as being creations of consciousness they also profoundly influence it. However, here is a different narrative: that of consciousness telling a story of its own origins and development—of itself.

While objectivity of self-examination is scarcely possible this is not so with regard to a subjective expression of consciousness—and this is, we suggest, what the histories of art, music, literature, religion, folk lore, fairy tales, alchemy etc. are largely concerned with. In these, consciousness expresses its own experience and even reflects on itself via a multitude of symbolic forms. Symbols are the vehicles of consciousness so that it can articulate its own experience and nature. Consciousness has to examine itself through symbols that require interpretation. It tells stories, which become ever deeper reflections on its own self. Mankind's eyes open with the birth of ego, a separate self, a distinct discriminating consciousness, to observe that which is outside. But this world is also a construction of our own consciousness which is ultimately enmeshed in it. Fully aware consciousness is the flower of evolution, a capacity of creation to evolve an intelligence to reflect back on itself.

Homo sapiens, despite an extraordinary development of consciousness, forever struggles with an animal inheritance. One of the decisive changes in our cultural evolution is the transition from the Great Mother to patriarchal religions—a new dominant in consciousness. The worship of the Great Mother was essentially that of the mysteries of nature of which our animal inheritance was part. The sky gods of the patriarchy, representing the birth of a transcendent, individualistic, and moralistic consciousness, tried to control our own animal instincts and opposed the immersion of consciousness within nature.

There are numerous myths concerning the struggle of this transition to a different stage of consciousness from the world of nature to civilisation, the most common being heroic battles against ferocious animals, the archetype of which is the dragon. While the individual significance of this may be obvious—most of us have to struggle with our animal nature—it has also collective meaning in the history of our species. The dragon above all symbolises the Great Mother herself. This is a distorted projection of patriarchal consciousness. From the viewpoint of the emerging, individualised consciousness the danger is of being devoured by the unconsciousness which now becomes negatively imagined as the dragon. The great treasure of the developing Self, individualised and higher consciousness, cannot be released until the dragon is killed. Consciousness is in conflict with its own foundations.

The bull-fight is also a symbol of this theme of man versus nature. The bull has always been recognised as a tremendous force of nature. The history of a sacred, sacrificial relationship to this animal has been part of human history from its very beginnings, since it clearly represents man's relationship to his own instinctual nature and can be illustrated in three stages that shade into one another, overlap, and sometimes conflict. These stages are those of worship, prohibition, and battle.

Worship of the bull. The images on the walls of the Palaeolithic caves (40,000 years ago onwards) show many bulls, as wells as cows, which were clearly an object of fascination for early mankind—embodiments of fertility and power. In Ancient Egypt the worship of the bull (Apis) was one of the lengthiest traditions of animal worship stretching back thousands of years to early Egyptian civilisation. Individual, real-life bulls were worshipped as deities and believed to be incarnations of Osiris. Ancient Egypt represents a decisive movement to the patriarchy, yet many of its religious practices and beliefs were transmitted from tribal customs that went back into time immemorial. Egypt is thus a mixture of opposites, between the Great Mother and patriarchal gods, between worship of the forces and creatures of the earth on the one hand, and sun worship on the other—not surprising given the longevity of its civilisation. Bull worship, the embodiment of the god in fertility and power, was a central element of this transmission. In Egypt we record also the first signs of bull sacrifice. From Egypt, bull worship and sacrifice spread around the Mediterranean, which was not difficult since the fascination with, and awe at, this force of nature is universal. For example, in Minoan Crete, popularly associated with goddess worship, the frescoes of the palaces were adorned with sporting youths, male and female, leaping over the horns of bulls.

It is not difficult to imagine the power and fertility rites associated with these acrobatics, these leaps over death into life. The frescos depict a *leaping* not a *fighting* ritual; not an effort to conquer and kill but to partake in a fertility ritual in which life and death forces are closely linked. This is far closer to bull worship. Here we have a civilisation much closer to the world of nature than, say, the Hebrews and the Greeks who show a decisive transition, a movement away from mankind's immersion in nature and its implied dominance of the Great Mother. The sacrificing of bulls to the gods existed in these times, but this sacrifice was precisely because these animals were of such importance.

Prohibition of bull worship. As the patriarchal Abrahamic religions developed, the immersion in nature and its mysteries was prohibited—clearly documented in the Old Testament, for example in the Book of Leviticus. The Judaic religion developed out of, and then in opposition to, the nature religions that surrounded them. The goddess worship of the Canaanites (bordering the Jewish tribes) was forbidden and there was always a danger of the Jews falling back into the sexuality, licentiousness, and promiscuity they perceived in such religions, represented by worship of fertility symbols, of which the bull or the cow were prime examples. When Moses went up to the mount to receive the tablets of stone with the law written upon them (Exodus 32, 33) the Jews below returned to the worship of the golden calf. Upon his return Moses organised the slaughter of three thousand people in punishment for this betrayal of Yahweh. The Abrahamic religions subsequently set themselves against the worship of the Great Mother and saw this battle against her as one that defined their civilisation.

Battle against nature and the bull. There are many myths concerning the battle against monsters and animals by the emerging heroes of patriarchal civilisation. The battle against the dragon is of course famous, but those against the bull exist also from the start of these civilisations and are still with us today. They encapsulate a story, in mythic form, of the transition from one stage of consciousness to another, from one type of civilisation to another.

Figure 16. Bull fighting.
A stage in man's relation to instincts.

In Greek mythology the legend of the Minotaur tells a tale of this transition. The Mediterranean island of Crete was the centre of Minoan civilisation, situated geographically and culturally between Egypt and Greece. It had long traditions of worship of female snake goddesses as well as the bull-jumping events referred to above. We may think of it as transitional between the Great Mother and the patriarchal gods. Minos was a famous king of Crete, Parsiphae his wife. Legend has it that Parsiphae fell into a passion with a beautiful white bull and persuaded Daedalus, the master craftsman, to construct a likeness of a cow, into which she entered so as to copulate with it. The offspring of this union was the Minotaur, half-man, half-bull. Minos, on advice from the oracle at Delphi, had Daedalus construct a labyrinth at the centre of which the Minotaur was incarcerated. Parallel to these events, King Minos, as the most powerful king of the Mediterranean, demanded as tribute from Athens seven of their sons and daughters to be sent at intervals as sacrifice to the Minotaur. On the third occasion, Theseus, in the mould of the hero, was one of the group to be sacrificed but he vowed to kill the Minotaur. On his arrival in Crete Minos' daughter, Ariadne, fell in love with him and armed him with a sword for this task. She also gave him the famous thread by which to find his way out of the labyrinth. Theseus, with this help, slew the Minotaur and led his companions to freedom.

The legend, for our purposes, illustrates the shift from the world of nature immersion to that of reason and the "higher" spirit embodied in Greece—a movement to patriarchal consciousness. The Minoan culture of Crete, halfway between Isis and Olympus, is balanced between the old world of mother worship and the new patriarchal civilisations such as Greece. The old world is connected to Egypt and from there back into time immemorial to Africa where mankind was identified with the world of nature. The Minoan goddesses, holding the snakes of instinct and rebirth, represent a world quite different from the emerging rationalisms, scientific speculation, and "higher" philosophies of Greece, the emerging paradigm of rational consciousness.

The prelude to the Minotaur story is of a conflict between Minos and his wife. She threatened his masculine rule with her union with the bull, symbol of fertility, sexuality, and power, the essence of the old world. Minos' requirement that the Athenians sacrifice their sons and daughters to the half-bull of Crete is a demand for sacrifice and submission of the Greek world to the old world of nature worship. Minos himself, like Minoan civilisation, is also clearly in a halfway position between two worlds. Theseus, like other Greek heroes, gained freedom for himself and his community by liberation from the Great Mother, the world of nature, by slaying the half-bull half-man.

The violence of the struggle against our animal nature and the desire to conquer it is shown in the above myths and stories. This theme continues with Roman civilisation, which followed the Greek. Arthur Toynbee in his *Study of History* (1939–61) suggests that if an observer of the third century Roman Empire were to hazard a guess as to the future dominant religion the bets would have been on Mithraism, with many hundreds of centres of worship in Rome, very popular throughout the Roman Empire, and widely followed in the Roman legions. The central motif of this religion, found in its places of worship, was the killing of a bull (tauroctony).

Figure 17. Mithras.
Mithras to the sun-god looks, the bull falls to the soil.
The world of instinct now repressed, nature is despoiled.

Stemming originally from Persian origins the Roman versions show Mithras looking over his shoulder at Sol, the sun-god, and killing an exhausted bull who is being tortured by other wild animals. Although the Mithraic cult is shrouded in mystery it fits well into the theme of these pages. The emerging patriarchal civilisations and religions violently opposed those of the Great Mother. Her symbols from the animal kingdom, be they dragon, snake, or bull, are killed in their mythologies. The new solar gods of light and "higher" consciousness fight a battle to destroy the Great Mother and her worship. The world of nature, as it emerges instinctively with the psyche of mankind, is violently attacked. Solar mythology (achievement, individuality, higher consciousness, discipline, conquest, male values, higher reason, and the light) replaces the female and lunar (cyclical rebirth, world of nature, the collective, instincts, and reproduction). The history of human consciousness is a creative-destructive evolution and clearly violent.

For those who find such speculation far-fetched, consider the bull fight which exists in Spain to this day. Where did it come from if not from these mythologies that were powerfully focussed in the Mediterranean? Why such elaborate ritual and drama in these bull killings? Does not this fight between man and bull represent an ancient ritual that has survived into modern times? Could it be the survival of a Mithraic mystery rite in a gladiatorial setting? The anthropologist Julian Pitt-Rivers (1954) suggests it is a Christian cult of the bull, "… that the Spanish bullfight recalls the Mithraic bull sacrifice, though under the aspect of Catholicism". The *torero* represents the solar hero, higher intelligence, and skill while the bull is the powerful and threatening world of nature that has to be mastered and slain. This is a fight of man against his "lower" instincts. In mythological terms it is the defeat of the Great Mother by the emerging solar civilisations of higher consciousness.

The freeing of our ego consciousness from the grip of the dragon of the unconscious is only part of the drama (Neumann, 1989). This battle is also the freeing of the higher self from the suffocating grip of nature. The hero, the individual consciousness about to fight the dragon, is the son of the creative spirit, belonging to the sky-gods, and this spirit must be liberated from its entrapment in nature. We have also a battle concerning the spiritual aspects of consciousness. Spirit had previously been embodied in nature and the Great Mother but is now to be "rescued" and "freed" from the dragon's embrace. Thus, the hero embodies the emergence of a higher form of consciousness or a higher personality. The treasure, or the maiden which the dragon guards, is to be released but controlled by the conquest of this monster.

However, there is a cost to this transition. While consciousness feels a sense of freedom, released from the confines of the unconscious, there is a price to pay for the separation from nature. Thus, Hercules neglects his wife and pays the price; Perseus kills the gorgon but is haunted by the furies; Oedipus slays his father and is blinded; Siegfried destroys the dragon, frees the treasure, and gains Brunhilde, only to be tricked and destroyed by his own dark nature and sexual impulses. It is impossible to do violence to our own nature (slay the dragon, kill the monster) without paying a price such as guilt, sorrow, loss, alienation, and division within ourselves. Moreover, if the dragon represents our own inner nature then it follows it cannot be destroyed but only repressed and, as Freud poignantly noted, the repressed has a habit of returning. Thus, we can expect that the Great Mother, in the form of the dragon, will return within the Abrahamic religions, her greatest enemy, to wreak vengeance. And this is precisely what happens in Revelation, the last book of the bible.

While *Homo sapiens* evolved *circa* 200,000 years ago in East Africa, it was not until *circa* 50,000 years ago that sufficient artefacts were preserved to give us no doubt as to the emergence of humanity. The astounding cave paintings of France and Spain (but also other parts of the world) illustrate that from 40,000 years ago *Homo sapiens* possessed a higher self and awareness, an aesthetic and most probably spiritual sensibility. From this period we have the first preserved musical instruments, flutes made of bird bone and mammoth tusk, some exquisitely made, as well as more sophisticated weaponry and tools. Great Mother worship existed, we suspect, in Europe since 20,000 BCE, where there were (and some still preserved) wonderful figurines of female reproductive power—surely the emergence of the mother goddess. From about 10,000 BCE, the Neolithic agricultural revolution grasped the secret of crop production. There existed from this time a mixture of Great Mother worship and male gods, eventually crystallising in patriarchal religions and civilisations which emerged from 5,000–2,000 BCE in Egypt, India, China, and later (500 BCE) in Greece and Rome. There were, then, pulses of patriarchal religions and societies, at first coexisting with Great Mother worship, at times cohabiting, then replacing and dominating the Great Mother nature spirit.

The establishment of civilisation, especially in its patriarchal form, was, then, a decisive movement and development of human consciousness. The attitude of this evolving consciousness to its own self, especially to its own platform of creatureliness or animality, is played out in mythology, and some of its forms are the relationship of human to animal and of man to woman, behind which is the relationship to nature. Concerning this distinction between two types of consciousness—that of patriarchal civilisation and that of one more immersed in nature—an illustrative analogy is Melanie Klein's model of the stages of psychological development of the infant. As already mentioned, she characterises the earliest stage as paranoid-schizoid in which the opposites of the good and the bad breast dominate the psyche, which is split between polar experiences of benevolence and frustration in relationship to the mother upon whom the child is totally dependent. The child has little or no ego to defend himself against dark feelings of anger and envy. He is also capable of being overjoyed by the love of the mother. The stage is called paranoid-schizoid because, in Klein's view, both paranoid (intensely fearful and suspicious) and schizoid (being split by opposites) features dominate the early psyche. This is a useful model for the psyche of early man. *Participation mystique,* the enwrapment in nature, is not just the experience of bliss, any more than a child experiences solely happiness with the mother. *Participation mystique* is a non-egoic state in which the opposites of the human psyche are experienced with tremendous intensity; one in which the psyche moves its centre from one pole to the opposite dramatically and quickly—a borderline phenomenon. The stabilising force of the ego, reasoning with the psyche, calming its fears and warning of its excessive emotion, is not strong in the early psyche. Thus, brutality and savagery could exist easily in the same person along with love or tenderness. The opposites are not experienced as a problem because there is little reflecting ego to be agonised by them—there is the *experiencing* as opposed to the *reflective* subject.

As the new more individualised and "higher" consciousness liberates itself from the world of nature, from the enmeshment in the Great Mother, as there is a shift to patriarchal consciousness, to sky-gods, principles, spirit, and even to ideas of one transcendent god, there is a sense of elation and power. Man rejoices in a new freedom of mind and feels a solar status, a universality, and immortality soaring above the earth to the heavens, no longer grounded by instinct and traditions of the group, but destined to produce order and civilisation. The firmly established consciousness begins to rejoice in its power and individuality; it now has a more distinct and robust ego. It also has a higher self while it attempts to control its "lower" animal nature.

Yet, no sooner have patriarchal religions gained ascendancy than the awareness of an enormous loss becomes evident. Notions of evil and sin also become common. Consciousness expresses these feelings mythologically. The new creation myths, the narratives that shape the consciousness of the patriarchy, express these conflicts in great myths of creation, how evil came into the world, the fall of mankind, the place of man and woman in the God's creation, their responsibilities, and the dangers they face. In the next three sections we examine these themes in the creation mythology of the Hebrew bible.

CHAPTER ELEVEN

The Garden of Eden

Adam and Eve Hear the Heavenly Words of Caution

Love is sweet and love is pure,
A light within your soul.
Fragrance melts your outer core
Surrender to be whole.
Forever and forever more
This love transcends all time.
Your bodies do one soul unite
As words are sung in rhyme.

Your bodies melt within its flame,
Soft the essence, tender touch.
New day dawns this kiss is all,
You can hardly bear so much.
By nature blessed your hearts do ache,
Be at peace and still your mind.
Here's creation for your sake,
All is given to mankind.

The joy within creation's light
May be your only guide.
Rejoice in every moment
There's nothing you should hide.
You are perfect, you are whole,
There's nothing left to need.
All you want lies in you now,
Already you are freed.

Oh, why seek more when what you have
Can last for all earth's time?
Why seek for knowledge evermore?
It only ends in crime. Against yourself against the world,
Forgo this path of woe.
Already you have wholeness,
There's nothing more to know.

Love within is all there is,
No need is there to search
For monuments of earthly pride,
Why try to build a church?
No need for armies or for pride,
Why seek you for respect?
All that you could want is here,
There's no need to reflect.

Just be quiet, soft and still,
Hark to nature's voice.
Harmony's within your soul,
No need to make a choice.
Avoid the tree of knowledge,
Ask not the reason why.
Let not the serpent tempt you,
Its fruit will make you die.

No need to take the apple,
No knowledge you require.
Stay full in this existence,
Just quieten your desire.
Why seek to know the difference
Between what's right and wrong?
This Garden has eternal life,
It's here where you belong.

Figure 18. The Garden of Eden.

In this transition to civilisation consciousness, at first, feels relatively freed from its enmeshment in nature and rises to new heights. But there is a cost to this new-found power. In loss we realise the value of the irreplaceable and thus construct images of a lost paradise, such as the biblical Garden of Eden in which man and woman lived in love and harmony with a benevolent creator. We lament the loss of what we feel we have destroyed.

Psychologically, the Book of Genesis, the bible's opening great myth, concerns the birth of consciousness of our species, which is the bearer of a unique seed that has lain in creation and is now about to unfold its beautiful, mysterious, and dark flower.

Let us look on this founding myth of the Abrahamic religions from a mythological, psychological, and evolutionary perspective. The opening lines of Genesis tell of a birth from the darkness of the deep, the unconscious, the millions of years of evolution in which life had been unaware of itself. There is differentiation, above from below, and the waters from the land. "Let there be light" declares the central event of this creation, the origins of consciousness itself, of divine making. The division of the world into animals and life of all kinds is the further development of this consciousness that is now capable of differentiating and naming the individual parts of this creation—that is to say mankind becomes aware of the world.

The biblical myth suggests that we lived in harmony with a benevolent creator. Man and woman lived in unison and were at one with nature. Despite an idyllic existence, with the promptings of Lucifer, we chose to taste the only forbidden fruit in this Garden of Eden upon pain of death, that of the Tree of Knowledge—that is, we "chose" consciousness rather than remain in the unconscious. In punishment for this and to prevent us reaching the Tree of Life, we were banished from the Garden to an inferior existence, our earthly condition, from which we long to return to the state of union we have lost—that is, the cost of our consciousness is the loss of the state of unity in nature and the unconscious. The source of such a myth, and many others like it, is threefold.

First, in the collective unconscious of our species is an awareness of the loss of a primal, original state of union before ego consciousness, when instead we were part of a great whole. Collectively, the Garden of Eden, represents a state prior to developed ego consciousness, which appears, in retrospect, as a state of oneness, a unity with nature and within ourselves. It is the unconscious before the emergence of an individualised ego consciousness that is aware of its isolation. By the birth of our ego consciousness we have broken from a larger unity of which we were once part. The Tree of Knowledge of good and evil is our emerging ego consciousness, about to differentiate from the unconscious, which produces the awareness of death, the separation from the original unity. The collective ego consciousness of our species, like that of an infant, is at first fragile and easily returns to the mother, the unconscious. It then strengthens until it can apparently gain independence, from which position it may look back at previous stages, such as childhood, as a lost paradise. The myth therefore represents our own consciousness and its experience of itself. Adam and Eve are the universal human beings, our primal selves, our essence; the Garden is the state of unconsciousness from which we evolved; the Tree of Knowledge is ego consciousness which must rupture the early state of unity in the unconscious; Lucifer, the bringer of light, therefore represents this drive towards consciousness. The Tree of Life is the second tree in the Garden. God fears that Adam and Eve, who have already become like gods, in that they are now aware of good and evil, will also taste its fruit and become as himself. This symbol of the second tree, to be explored shortly, has its chief significance in the potential higher development of our species and of all individuals.

Second, individually, we respond to such myths, since we carry a memory of union with our mothers in our infancy—a template of all love. The myth represents the state of love we crave, be it personal or spiritual, from which we feel separated. This is our personal Garden of Eden, the unity and love that is the basis of a natural, healthy existence, from which we differentiate into individualised beings via our ego consciousness. Yet, we long to return to this state all our lives and to this end we seek union with another human being.

Third spiritually, by virtue of our ego consciousness, we feel cast down into our lower selves and separated from the bliss of union, our higher selves. We are trapped in a state of conflict, division, shame, and guilt, knowing that there is within us a state of wholeness, of oneness, that we wish to be united with again. Once having experienced the state of unity, life in its conflicted state appears like a fall from grace. We also seek this state of bliss, unity, and love in spiritual experience, as well as searching for rejuvenation, beauty, and healing energy in nature. Thus, we have a yearning for the Garden of Eden, which expresses itself in many forms, for instance in our love experience, in spiritual union, artistic expression, and appreciation for the beauty of the earth.

Consciousness is built on the rupture of its emergence from the unconscious, and, as such, subsequently unconsciously expresses itself in compensation for this trauma. The creative act of the emergence of consciousness is dependent on the repression of our unconscious, an inevitable act but with potentially destructive consequences. Subsequently, consciousness attempts to heal the wound of its origins.

As a mythological representation the Garden of Eden is condensed metaphor and symbol. Many layers of human experience, feeling, and intuition are compacted in a single narrative and this myth tells a story, which among other things represents the consciousness of a particular culture at a certain stage of its development. It can even represent the prejudices of a civilisation. It can show the structural mytho-psychological underpinnings of a whole attitude to life, in this case one that saturates the attitudes and beliefs of three powerful religions, the Judaic, the Christian, and the Islamic.

The more a myth spans cultures and time the greater its impact, significance, and universality. The myth of Genesis underpinned the Abrahamic religions and therefore had enduring importance in the Near East and the West. Do these myths have any significance in the light of scientific knowledge? There is now ample evidence for the age of the universe and the earth. There is also a powerful scientific paradigm of evolution with extraordinary explanatory power that has revolutionised our understanding of the development of life. We possess a fossil record going back millions of years that reveals that mankind did, indeed, evolve from primates. From this point of view Genesis cannot be literally true yet this myth was believed in its totality and down to minute detail for the length of Christian, Judaic, and Islamic civilisations. It is only the development of free thinking, independent of church and religion, that provided humanity with a new knowledge of the origins and evolution of the cosmos, the earth, and life. In the West the early glimpses of the existence of evolution occurred in the relatively free thought of Ancient Greece (Anaximander, Xenophanes, Plato, Socrates, and Aristotle among many others), then much later in Western Europe from the seventeenth century (for example,

John Ray, 1686; Carolus Linnaeus, 1735; Comte de Buffon, 1749; Pierre-Louis Moreau de Maupertuis, 1751; Charles Bonnet, 1770; Erasmus Darwin, 1794; Jean-Baptiste Lamarck, 1809; Charles Darwin, 1808). Hinduism has had far fewer problems adapting to modern science than the Judaic-Christian tradition. Scientific discoveries of the age of the universe or the evolution of life on earth are not problematic for Hindus, since this is anticipated in their mythology and cosmologies.

It is the argument of Jungian psychology, demonstrated not only by Jung but by many others of his school, including E. Neumann, that the value of myths lies not in explanations of the outer world but in symbolic representations of the nature of consciousness itself. Once it is accepted that it is impossible to take Genesis literally then it must be disassociated from scientific investigation. Its truth lies in the realm of symbol. It tells an inner story, much as a fairy tale, dream, parable, or legend does, which is not to do with analytic investigation but is rather concerned with an intuitive, symbolic exploration of the inner world and consciousness itself. It is the symbolic representation of the emergence of consciousness from the point of view of a particular civilisation.

CHAPTER TWELVE

Lucifer

Lucifer fell high from heaven,
In his pride did he choose.
Challenged he the supreme power,
Mighty battle did he lose.
Clothed in darkness was he cast out,
Down fell he upon the earth.
Fallen angels his companions,
Here was he at mankind's birth.

The impulse into consciousness,
The bringer of the light.
Dread serpent in the garden,
He knows what's wrong and right.
With fruit of Tree of Knowledge
He tempted Mother Eve,
"Taste this apple if you dare,
Great knowledge you receive."

But Eve at first was cautious,
"This fruit must not be ate.
If our God we do deceive,
Then death will be our fate.
The fruits of all this garden
Are waiting to be picked,
Except the Tree of Knowledge
It is forbidden strict."

But Lucifer persisted now,
More weight he brought to bear:
"As gods on high you will become
Your self becomes aware.
Taste this fruit, become divine,
A world you can create.
Your eyes they will be opened wide,
From slumber you awake."

Thus Eve did take the apple
Which Adam too did taste.
In consciousness they both awoke,
Heaven closed its gate.
So, which of these two arguments
Proves to have more weight?
Now death and knowledge co-exist:
Emprisoned freedom is our fate.

Figure 19. Lucifer falls high from heaven.

The human creature who has fallen from the garden is the bearer of an extraordinary consciousness but one that is full of suffering and conflict. Why? Our consciousness is beset by distortions, conflicts, inner divisions, compulsions, addictions, and dissatisfactions. Why? This consciousness, extraordinary though it may be, is far from being content with itself and is compelled to continually seek external fulfilment and achievement. Why? Throughout most of our history we have made sacrifices to gods to appease their anger, to persuade them to favour us, to say sorry for our sins—such guilt and shame. Why? Human beings are, and always have been, the perpetrators of enormous amounts of "evil". Why? We are obsessed with death. Why? There is so much unhappiness, yet we have so much? Why? The answer to these questions lies in the shadow of consciousness—its darkness.

We will explore these themes through the biblical myth of the temptation and fall set out in Genesis. Myths are symbolic representations and are the best way to express such complexity. Great myths are archetypal and therefore tell, in symbolic and often narrative form, the struggles and dilemmas of consciousness and the human predicament. The theory of evolution, by contrast, is very much concerned with precise knowledge of the external world. When did the universe begin—exactly? How long has there been life on the planet—exactly? When did *Homo sapiens* appear—exactly? The myths care nothing about exact time, causation, or reasoning, for that matter. They are timeless, acausal, and metaphysical, beyond and above, therefore, the "reality" of our reasoning mind. They tell an inner story of human consciousness rather than the outer story of the origin or development of the world.

The shadow of consciousness, its darkness, is explored in two stages. The first is the fall for which Lucifer is held responsible in the Bible. The second is the appearance of Satan, of evil in mankind's consciousness. The biblical myth of the temptation and fall set out in Genesis is our initial vehicle and we interpret the archetypes of both Lucifer and Satan psychologically. We examine Lucifer first, while Satan will be for a later chapter.

Lucifer was the chief of the angels and in some interpretations it is suggested that in his pride he challenged God and was ejected from heaven (Ezekiel 28:12–18, Luke 10:18). Dante, John Milton, and William Blake used this myth to great effect, since it has great resonance in the Christian tradition. Thus, like Adam and Eve, Lucifer, the light bringer (the meaning of the name in Latin), the morning star, the bringer of consciousness, is punished by a violent separation from the divine. Lucifer is the impulse to consciousness out of the primal unity, the drive for differentiation, the birth of a new world, of conscious discrimination, separated self-awareness. This identification of Lucifer with the light can more easily be understood as the consciousness impulse and the breaking from the primal unity. A passage of the Old Testament declares: "How art thou fallen from heaven, O Lucifer, son of the morning?" (Isaiah 14:12)

The temptation scene in Genesis has a powerful seed of symbolic truth wrapped within the defensive husk of Judaic moralistic consciousness, which was obsessed with sexuality and obedience.

The text of Genesis opens the drama:

> Now the serpent was more subtil than any beast of the field which the Lord God had made. And he said unto the woman, Yea, hath God said, Ye shall not eat of every tree of the garden?

> And the woman said unto the serpent, We may eat of the fruit of the trees of the garden. But of the fruit of the tree which is in the midst of the garden, God hath said, Ye shall not eat of it, neither shall ye touch it, lest ye die. And the serpent said unto the woman, Ye shall not surely die. For God doth know that in the day ye eat thereof, then your eyes shall be opened, and ye shall be as gods, knowing good and evil. And when the woman saw that the tree was good for food, and that it was pleasant to the eyes, and a tree to be desired to make one wise, she took of the fruit thereof, and did eat, and gave also unto her husband with her; and he did eat. And the eyes of them both were opened, and they knew that they were naked; and they sewed fig leaves together, and made themselves aprons.
>
> (Genesis 3:1)

Comments. Lucifer is most subtle of all creatures, outwardly characterised as treacherous (the form of serpent) and subtle (cunning, underhand, devious). But Lucifer is the inevitable impulse to consciousness, which has to rupture the primal unity of unconscious identity. As serpent he is the primal, instinctual energy that pushes to higher forms of consciousness in evolution (or kundalinic energy in Hindu meditational practices)—he is therefore subtle (the giver of knowledge) and treacherous (this impulse to consciousness will undermine the primal unity). He is, nevertheless, part of God's creation. This "scheme", this drama, is inevitable. Consciousness is the paradoxical product of creation. In the terminology of this book, the immanence of the universe expresses itself in the birth trauma of consciousness.

Eve prepares the drama to come. In paradise they have everything, all the fruits, except one, in the midst of the garden, the taste of which is death. In the primal unconscious nothing is lacking—there is no ego to feel a lack; we are enfolded in the great primal unconscious. The tree in the garden which is forbidden is consciousness. If one becomes a conscious separate being, an ego, then one dies to previous existence contained in the womb of creation. This primal unity must die; it is ruptured by the emergence of consciousness.

Life evolved for millions of years without self-consciousness being developed in any animal. Let us suppose that consciousness is immanent in evolution, not programmed as an inevitability, since many circumstances may conspire against it. But higher forms of consciousness and eventually self-consciousness will emerge in the course of evolution when conditions are ripe, like a seed falling on fertile ground. Within our current evolutionary perspective, the vast preconscious period can be thought of as a Garden of Eden, this earth a paradise. The emergence of *Homo sapiens* is the birth of consciousness symbolised by this tree in the midst of the garden that inexorably emerges from this earth/paradise. It does not matter if one believes in evolution or creation, the paradox of the emergence of consciousness is the same.

Lucifer, the consciousness impulse, replies that Adam and Eve will not die, that on the contrary they will be as gods, knowing good and evil, that is, that they will emerge into consciousness, have knowledge and discrimination, will awake from the slumber of the unconscious; no longer be just another part of creation but will "know" it and "know" themselves. Therefore they will be as gods—not as God the creator, but as gods that are distinct from lower creation that is not self-aware. Self-awareness is semi-divine, an extraordinary product of creation/evolution.

Eve eats the fruit—it is good, "to be desired" and "to make one wise", that is, it brings consciousness. She gives it to Adam who also tastes this fruit. The movement to consciousness takes place in stages: temptation, persuasion, partial conviction, then total acceptance. It is a transition full of conflict and drama.

One of the many powerful themes compacted in the temptation of the Eve story is that the emergence of consciousness is a moral problem. Genesis is saturated with a moral dimension. The very existence of consciousness is a moral dilemma. Why?

From the start, the serpent is characterised as untrustworthy, dangerous to the well-being of paradise, to Adam and Eve, and therefore to this creation. Eve's first words are of a moral restriction with the most severe penalty—they are to taste the fruit in the midst of the Garden on pain of death. Lucifer immediately challenges this, saying that on the contrary they will be as gods and their eyes will be opened—that is, God has lied to them. But both these positions are true. On eating the fruit Eve finds it to be "good" rather than death-giving. After sharing it with Adam, however, indeed their eyes are opened, they realise they are naked and are ashamed. The unity with their creator is finished; they hide from him in guilt. However, the awareness and anguish of death, the sundering of the primal unity, now comes into the world. Consciousness and death are inextricably linked.

An infant does not realise she is naked. She is not aware of herself. Adam and Eve were at first as infants. Their emergence into self-consciousness is to become aware of themselves as separate beings, no longer one with the mother, or the garden, or God's paradise. Consciousness is presented as a crime against nature. From this perspective self-awareness is an amazing and totally abnormal event, one, moreover, which we will see more clearly later, puts nature, this garden, this earth, into great danger.

The emergence of consciousness, in the biblical myth, is accompanied by shame and guilt; a great loss occurred, and the consequence is great punishment. Interpreting this narrative as the birth of consciousness the story makes sense even from the evolutionary perspective. The biblical story continues:

> And they heard the voice of the Lord God walking in the garden in the cool of the day: and Adam and his wife hid themselves from the presence of the Lord God amongst the trees of the garden. And the Lord God called unto Adam, and said unto him, Where art thou? And he said, I heard thy voice in the garden, and I was afraid, because I was naked; and I hid myself. And he said, Who told thee that thou wast naked? Hast thou eaten of the tree, whereof I commanded thee that thou shouldest not eat? And the man said, The woman whom thou gavest to be with me, she gave me of the tree, and I did eat. And the Lord God said unto the woman, What is this that thou hast done? And the woman said, The serpent beguiled me, and I did eat.
>
> (Genesis 3:8)

Adam and Eve now hide from the Lord, since shame and doubt of a separated discriminatory consciousness cannot bear the light of wholeness, or bear the loss of the unity from which they came. Consciousness is linked to shame. However, inevitably, we are called to account for this state of consciousness we are in. Our own desire for wholeness makes this demand. Adam admits the fear, shame, and guilt of his consciousness in front of the totality. God demands to know what they have done to be in this forbidden state of self-awareness. Although they are now aware, they do not know why they aware. They are unaware of the purpose, if any, of this awareness. Ego consciousness is unaware of its ultimate *raison d'être*. Adam blames Eve. Eve blames the serpent. After guilt and shame comes blame. The ultimate cause is apparently the serpent, the treacherous Lucifer, the consciousness impulse itself.

Judaism, Christianity, and Islam have always had a fundamental theological problem. If there is one source of everything, one good God that has created the universe, then how does darkness and evil exist? The answer of Augustine, in the fifth century, believed by Christians for over 1000 years, is that evil has no independent existence, it is merely the absence of good—the doctrine of *privatio boni*. Yet, in Judaic mythology, there is only one creator. Somehow he must be ultimately responsible for what is in the universe or he must be much more complex than we imagined. If he is the totality, then this darkness must be him. He might be split and have radically different sides to himself. Or is it we, in our consciousness, that have divided the totality into separate halves? Lucifer, from this viewpoint, is the split-off part of the Godhead—split by our consciousness.

Since this myth is at the foundation of Judaism, passed on to Christianity and Islam, we may observe its many consequences, developing like leitmotifs in the symphony of Western and Near Eastern consciousness—the doctrine of original sin, the fallen state of humanity, the necessity for redemption, the misogyny that saturated these cultures, to name but a few. The biblical myth of the origins of the world is really a myth of the origin of consciousness, actually, to be specific, the origins of the consciousness of patriarchal religions and their civilisations, those that believed in a transcendent, moral God. It was written around 800–500 BC and is the most radical myth of the emerging patriarchal religions and civilisations of this time. Nature, sexuality, and reproduction are repressed and henceforward regarded as evil. It is founded on a severe rupture from the mythologies of the Great Mother that now constituted the repressed unconscious of the emerging patriarchal psyche.

CHAPTER THIRTEEN

Banishment

Get ye gone O wretched sinners,
From this garden banished be.
Tree of Knowledge now is tasted,
Suffer hence your destiny.
Consciousness is now awakened,
Self-awareness is your fate.
Constant guilt is your companion,
Time from now is getting late.

Labour now is your obsession,
Count its long hours all your days.
Fear of hunger ever drives you,
Now you keep the wolf at bay.
Paths of knowledge must be taken
Once you've tasted of its fruit.
Blind you are, you go on searching,
Feeling safe is your pursuit.

Tree of Life is strict forbidden,
Way is barred by flaming sword.
Greater knowledge is quite hidden,
Weep, repent unto your Lord.

Unity with your creator
Now is sundered, all seems doomed.
Consciousness is now shame-ridden
Pained by anguish of its wound.

Into death you shall be banished,
Pain and anguish be your lot.
From here on your days are numbered,
'Scape from judgement you cannot.
Darkness now your mind will cover,
Over earth then will you roam.
Heart in sadness will hence suffer,
You are aliens in your home.

But know this secret, fallen earthlings,
Not entirely lost you are.
Great the gifts that you are given,
In you is a guiding star.
Set your compass to this true light,
Bear your loss and weep your tears,
You have a heart, you have a soul.
Still your mind, calm your fears.

Figure 20. Banishment.

Of Man's first disobedience, and the fruit
Of that forbidden tree whose mortal taste
Brought death into the World, and all our woe,
With loss of Eden, till one greater Man
Restore us, and regain the blissful Seat,
Sing, Heavenly Muse ...

—Milton. *Paradise Lost, Book 1*

The myth of the fall in the biblical tradition expresses an intuition that human consciousness emerged as a separation from a state of nature and the unconscious. A trauma occurred in Eden which led to the rupture of the primal unity leading to a banishment from the Garden. Paradoxically, we are both victims and perpetrators. On the one hand this happened to us, it was not our fault. On the other we willed it and therefore we are the cause.

The Garden of Eden, a state of fullness, of neither work nor worry, is replaced by a state of anxiety. How will one survive? One must labour, plan, toil, and bear sorrow. Anguish and guilt, sorrow and anger emerge. Defiance and exhilaration also occur as well as courage and stoicism. The human condition, for the Christian world, was founded on this original sin, which was inherited by every human being.

Such ideas are not confined to Jewish consciousness though the biblical myth is their most severe expression. By way of similarity, in Greek myth the Promethean act of stealing fire from the gods is punished. The myth tells of the Titan Prometheus who created mankind from clay and then, despite Zeus' prohibition, stole fire (consciousness) from the gods to bring these clay figures alive. For this punishable act Zeus sent Pandora's jar into the world to be opened with all its horrors. He also had Prometheus chained to a rock with an eagle eating his liver by day which regrew at night.

Both these myths, the Judaic and Greek, indicate that the achievement of consciousness is an act of defiance, as if a crime against nature. There are forces, prohibitions, in the myths against it. It brings dark consequences to the world and to man's psyche which now splits. There is also a distant hint that this is meant to be, that there must be a purpose in the banishment, this fall into consciousness. In the Greek myth Zeus feels threatened that his rule will end.

Prometheus

Prometheus the Titan bold
Olympus fire he stole.
The spark of our intelligence
With clay the human formed.
Then chained to rocks in punishment
For making race of men,
An eagle at his liver gorged,
That nightly grew again.

The paradox of consciousness,
A heavy price did bear.
In its birth there was a death,
With knowledge came despair.
At birth of human psyche
A deadly jar arrived.
Then curious Pandora
Opened it far wide.

But all the evils of this world
Within it were contained.
Once opened out they all did fly
And here they have remained.
The one exception to this fate
Was Hope the gods did send.
When all seems lost and we despair,
It stays our only friend.

The psyche is a mansion,
Its rooms have many names,
Some creation's greatest prize,
Others hell's domain.
You think you are the master,
That you're the morning star,
But don't forget the stolen fire
And fair Pandora's jar.

Figure 21. Prometheus steals the fire.

Zeus offers to free Prometheus if he will foretell what it is that will topple him. In the Christian story Adam and Eve are banished to prevent them eating the fruit of the second tree, the Tree of Life—as if Yahweh is threatened by this also. Consciousness breaks the *participation mystique*, the immersion of the psyche in nature and the enclosed system of the unconscious with its ruling dominants (fertility, power, reproduction, lunar cycles, rebirth etc.). At the same time mankind reaches for transcendent realisation (Tree of Life) but is prevented by Yahweh who now exiles them from Eden. Thus, transcendence, we suggest, is not available until the challenge of death is faced and therefore banishment into death awareness is a necessary development and fate.

In infant development this occurs psychologically as a break from the mother, a separation from the original state of oneness. Out of a dual unity, a separating consciousness centred in the ego develops. This template of a state of unity followed by a state of separation and division is universal in human experience because it symbolically tells a story of the birth of human consciousness of every individual.

It is also a frequent existential experience that we feel alienated from our own selves, from our deep nature, from the earth, and from the divine by virtue of our consciousness. Love, friendship, family systems, intimate relationships of all kinds are ways of trying to overcome this experience of separateness and isolation within our own being by creating a unity in love.

The text of Genesis continues …

> And the Lord God said unto the serpent, Because thou hast done this, thou art cursed above all cattle, and above every beast of the field; upon thy belly shalt thou go, and dust shalt thou eat all the days of thy life. And I will put enmity between thee and the woman, and between thy seed and her seed; it shall bruise thy head, and thou shalt bruise his heel.
>
> (Genesis 3:14)

Comment: sin comes into the world; the fallen state is one of punishment for an offence of humans against God; human consciousness is now split into opposition between its higher and lower nature.

> Unto the woman he said, I will greatly multiply thy sorrow and thy conception; in sorrow thou shalt bring forth children; and thy desire shall be to thy husband, and he shall rule over thee.
>
> (Genesis 3:16)

Comment: domination of the female by the male is legitimised—the female is seen as a danger to "higher" male consciousness. Consciousness further splits.

> And unto Adam he said, Because thou hast hearkened unto the voice of thy wife, and hast eaten of the tree, of which I commanded thee, saying, Thou shalt not eat of it: cursed is the ground for thy sake; in sorrow shalt thou eat of it all the days of thy life. Thorns also and thistles shall it bring forth to thee; and thou shalt eat the herb of the field. In the sweat of thy face

> shalt thou eat bread, till thou return unto the ground; for out of it wast thou taken: for dust thou art, and unto dust shalt thou return.
>
> (Genesis 3:17)

Comment: man was weak to listen to the female side of his nature; mankind is condemned to remain in consciousness; all humans are subject to this original sin inherited by the whole race; the primal unity is broken for ever; death awareness grips consciousness.

> And Adam called his wife's name Eve; because she was the mother of all living. Unto Adam also and to his wife did the Lord god make coats of skins, and clothed them.
>
> (Genesis 3:20)

Comment: Adam and Eve are our primal parents; the original sin will be inherited by all mankind; ego consciousness is universalised across the whole human race and therefore a break from the primal unity with the unconscious is its consequence; clothes are given to Adam and Eve to cover their shame since Judaic consciousness interprets the original sin as a sexual one, indicating the deep sexual repression of this culture. Nevertheless, it is also possible to interpret the above passage as having elements of love—Adam for his wife Eve, and the Lord for them both. Out of the pain of death comes the higher awareness of the response of love as the only answer.

> And the Lord god said, Behold, the man is become as one of us, to know good and evil: and now, lest he put forth his hand, and take also of the tree of life, and eat, and live for ever. Therefore the lord god sent him forth from the Garden of Eden, to till the ground from whence he was taken. So he drove out the man; and he placed at the east of the Garden of Eden cherubims, and a flaming sword which turned every way, to keep the way of the tree of life.
>
> (Genesis 3:22)

Comment: it now transpires that not one but two trees are forbidden in the Garden. The first was the Tree of Knowledge of good and evil, that is, the movement into consciousness. This already has god-like status. The second is the Tree of Life, an astounding new development, eternal life, we may suppose. To prevent mankind achieving this, Adam and Eve are twice-banished from the Garden. God's sentries, the cherubim with flaming swords, guard the Tree of Life.

Thus, the emergence into the life of consciousness, a defiant but creative act, is marred by death awareness. Life and death, creation and destruction, are the templates of our consciousness. Nature, this scheme of things, this evolution, the story of creation, is a mixture of opposites. The meaning of the Tree of Life can be seen within the context of the Abrahamic religions and particularly Christianity, although it is in many religions. It indicates that eternal life, which can be interpreted symbolically as the experience of wholeness, totality, and transcendence, is not available in earthly life, this consciousness. Christianity later modified this position by claiming that it is possible to pass through a vale of tears in this world to achieve heaven in the next. Thus, the possibility of eternal life is created by the death of Jesus Christ who opened the gates of hell so that souls could be released into heaven. These positions embody the severity of Judaism, Islam, and Christianity but are not typical of the East, where enlightenment is possible in this body, on this earth, where the eternal, the deathless, can be experienced as a spiritual state in this life. The Tree of Life (eternal life) is the possibility of transcendence, here and now, on this earth and in this consciousness. The reason why Adam and Eve are prevented from reaching the Tree of Life is that they (the human race) must pass through death-consciousness, the fallen state, before enlightenment is possible. We have, in the twentieth and twenty-first centuries, reached this decisive point in our evolution, since we can destroy all human, and perhaps all other life, on this planet. We are now on the verge of possible extinction and the death potential in our consciousness may now be realised by the technologies we possess. Only if we can pass through the gates of death and find a solution to our darkness can we achieve a transcendental connection to our destiny—the Tree of Life, the deathless state.

PART IV

THE FALLEN AND THE HIGHER STATES OF HUMANITY

Although human consciousness has evolved, developed, and changed over millennia the question remains: does it possess universal features? Chapter Three argued that there are universal structural features to our consciousness since we became fully human, outlining five evolved, overlapping and sometimes conflicting layers of our consciousness: animal inheritance, emotional structure, ego consciousness, the unconscious, and a higher consciousness, held together by the intelligence of the Self. But are there universal aspects of the functioning of consciousness? Our answer to this is yes—language, mathematics, for example, (but also in early humanity we always find religion, art, dance, singing, music, myth, cooking, games, and jokes). Beyond that, are there universal moral aspects to consciousness? Our answer to this is also yes. The creative and destructive, which we have presented as universal principles outside of ourselves, are also within the human psyche at every level, including the moral. Thus, the human capacity for negativity plus its capacity for higher consciousness and love are universal across the whole of human history, and are evident in the earliest myths that we have and are completely operational in contemporary individuals and societies. Part IV examines these universal components of our moral structure and argues that they are the result of the nature of our consciousness and its relation to the different parts of our psyche.

Chapter Fourteen explores how in the fallen state consciousness creates good and evil. The separated ego, as well as experiencing triumph, also suffers from limitation, division, emptiness, a sense of loss, and a fear of death. Envy, malignant thoughts, and evil emerge. In the Hebrew bible, the story of Cain and Abel, fratricide, is presented as the direct consequence of the fall.

Chapter Fifteen presents the Egyptian myth of Isis, Osiris, and Seth, which illustrates dramatically the origin of evil and the primal nature of the battle between the light and dark, good and evil. Like Cain and Abel, the battle between two brothers in the Egyptian myth demonstrates the centrality of shame (inferiority) and hatred in the human shadow and its contribution to negativity or "evil".

Chapter Sixteen examines evil and the shadow. Evil is the aggressive, destructive, and life-extinguishing parts of animal inheritance as they pass through the potentially distorted lens of human consciousness. Human beings, as evolved animals, share instincts, many appetites, passions, and fears with primates but our consciousness is a vast expansion of this inheritance and offers an arena for the enactment of our negativity.

Chapter Seventeen presents the higher self. Although fallen (separated from wholeness in a divided egoic state), humans are convinced they have a moral dimension, a capacity for higher awareness, and can raise themselves above carnal and destructive instincts; that they have a soul, and long to even transcend death. The higher self struggles with and often represses the darker animal and negative self. Thus, mankind is a divided creature yet with a capacity for integrative wholeness.

Chapter Eighteen argues that the experience of love is integral to human beings and, while evolving from our animal nature, is at the same time a manifestation of the higher self. It evolves out of the reproductive relations of our animal ancestors—sexual relationships, the love of mother and child, and family bonds. But with the emergence of human consciousness it expands outwards to others, to the world, to the universe, and inwards to an awareness of love within the self. It becomes a principle of all, the highest reality. It potentially redeems fallen mankind from separateness and the futility of vice.

CHAPTER FOURTEEN

The fallen state

When each of Adam's sons were born
He praised the Lord above.
To fill the void of Eden's loss
Sweet Eve gave all her love.
Raised were they unto the light
In hope for all our race.
Erase the memory of that pain,
The primal fall from grace.

Abel with their flocks kept watch,
While Cain did till the earth.
At common table took they food,
A bed they shared from birth.
At mother's breast they shared her milk,
They played at Adam's feet.
As boys they fought to pass the time,
In youth they did compete.

But darkness grew within Cain's soul,
He fought it hard and long.
Anger gripped him in a vice
To do his brother wrong.
For Abel seemed more favoured,
In all he did excel.
In parents' eyes he was their joy,
In shadow Cain did dwell.

In sacrifice to God above,
These brothers did light fires.
Cain brought corn and Abel sheep
Sought they favour in His sight.

The smoke rose straight from Abel's flame,
To heav'n his prayers ascend.
The fire but smouldered in Cain's hearth,
The wind the flame did bend.

And straight a fury Cain possessed,
A darkness like no other.
He roared in anger at the sky,
He leapt upon his brother.
And with a rock he broke his skull,
In body plunged a knife.
The blood cried sharp from out the ground
"Mankind is lost in strife."

The Lord of Cain demanded
"Wherefore is thy brother?
In dreadful anguish he is sought
By father and by mother.
If in love he is held dear,
Thou should be his seeker".
Cain replied from his dark soul,
"Am I my brother's keeper?"

"Exiled from this land and home
Thou must seek another.
A mark upon thy forehead be,
This man has killed his brother.
But no one shall molest thee,
Thy seed can grow full strong.
The mark of Cain is in mankind
In memory of this wrong."

Figure 22. Cain and Abel.

Mankind's fallen state is a result of the emergence of ego consciousness for which the word "fallen" is only partially accurate. Mankind also rises out of the unconsciousness in stages. His emergence in Africa around 200,000 years ago was just the beginning of a series of steps in which ego consciousness became more extensive and better established in the psyche and freed him from a state of unawareness. The Neolithic revolution and the subsequent move to the patriarchy were critical later stages in this process. Consciousness therefore escapes the clutches of the unconscious (the dragon) and experiences a sense of freedom.

On the other hand it experiences loss. It is with the patriarchal religions that the myth of a fallen state gathers force. Thus, we have a distinct feature of the human psyche. It is divided into various components that see and experience the world quite differently. The separated ego suffers from limitation, division, and an inner state of emptiness; shame is easily instilled into early consciousness; a sense of loss and a fear of death emerge. This sense of shame and anxiety is defended against; resentment and dissatisfaction emerge. Out of incompleteness and inadequacy, a sense of inferiority and a sense of envy arise that provoke destructive attack on goodness. Inner conflict based on inadequacy gives rise to malignancy. With the fall into ego consciousness mankind also becomes aware of a higher state, something divine within, which is projected into the heavens and the gods. However, dark envy and destructiveness attack this higher self. Thus, the myth of Lucifer's opposition to God, his pride that he was as "bright" and shining as the Creator, can also be interpreted as envy and malignant attack. Such a myth clearly strikes a response in the psyche since it is a symbolic narrative of one of its central dilemmas. This is the capacity of one part of the psyche (the envious and malignant) to attack and sometimes destroy the good part (the creative, loving, and bountiful). It has been persuasively suggested by Klein (2003) that envy and a subsequent attack of rage upon the mother is a common infant phantasy. This is primarily an intra-psychic phenomenon, a phantasy experienced within the psyche. This implies that the good parts of the psyche can be attacked enviously and with malevolence by other parts of itself. With this as an internal drama it is not difficult to imagine how it is projected on to others and the external world.

Chapter Four of Genesis, following the banishment of Adam and Eve from the Garden, opens with the birth of Cain and Abel, their two sons. Immediately their strife becomes apparent—the poem and illustration at the start of this chapter tell the tale. The consequences of the fall express themselves in our capacity to hate and destroy even our own family. Indeed, the common finding of psychotherapy is that the family is the chief locus and cause of the suffering and neuroses that beset us. Through the distortions, traumas, and afflictions to our attachments bonds, to our love, darkness enters the psyche and wreaks its damage. Cain is envious of Abel who seems more favoured in God's sight, a classic case of primal envy based on a sense of inferiority. Children are, as a rule, extraordinarily sensitive to their valuation in the family, and psychologically we might read this myth as a family drama. But the bible puts it in terms of a spiritual problem. Cain and Abel offer sacrifices to God to test his favour and it is the smoke from Abel's fire that rises straight while Cain's is blown adrift.

The forces of destruction within human beings can easily overwhelm those of order and reason. Many myths and legends concern a primal battle between light and darkness. To underestimate the darkness in our species is naive. However, it is instructive to realise that different cultures, while facing the same problem, view it differently. The radical answer given by the

Abrahamic religions is one version among others. Judaism was unconsciously influenced by Egyptian religion and mythology, even as it was consciously opposed. The Egyptians, however, had a less severe version of the creation of man and his fall, although there is disobedience and punishment as in the Judaic version. Unlike Yahweh, Ra, the Egyptian father god, is not the ultimate creator of the universe although he does create the earth. He emerged from the great waters (Nun), the unconscious, the primal oneness, as an egg. In his reign he creates mankind who, as he grows old, scorns and laughs at him. For this he sends the punishment of Hathor, the lion goddess, who slaughters many Egyptians. Thus, man's disobedience and disrespect is punished temporarily but this has none of the permanent, tragic severity that the fall of mankind has in the Judaic bible. Also, Ra's rule on earth has only a limited duration and he is replaced by Isis, who forces his secret power from him. Thus, we notice a female element entering the pantheon of Egyptian gods and this distinguishes it markedly from the Judaic tradition. Although Egypt was a patriarchy, with predominantly male heads of household and kingdoms, there was a strong female element in its culture. Isis, for example, was of immense popularity in Egyptian history across thousands of years, indicating a different attitude to life. However, the Egyptians certainly did not underestimate the brutality and psychopathy of evil in the human psyche. The next chapter examines in more detail the Egyptian view of evil, which, by contrast, throws light upon the Judaic-Christian-Islamic presentation.

CHAPTER FIFTEEN

Isis, Osiris, and Seth

At dawn before time's morning,
When all the gods were young,
Isis did Osiris love,
Though siblings they were one.
They danced across the heavens,
They sung among the stars,
Their love flowed sweet along the Nile,
It lived in trees and flowers.

Osiris had a brother Seth,
Hate consumed his heart.
Self-twisted fury eviled him,
A monster in the dark.
Two fundamental opposites
These brothers represent:
Seth malevolent violence,
Osiris innocence.

Exiled from their precious love
And in self-loathing wrapped,
Seth clothed himself in darkness,
Revenge his mind had trapped.
Osiris he did ambush,
Surprised him unaware.
The hunter lay in hiding,
Beguiled him in a snare.

Seth cruel stormed, Osiris shocked,
Across the skies they rushed.
Mediterranean gasped in wonder,
Saharan sands lay hushed.
The Atlas boomed their clash of swords,
Along the coast they raged.
The thunder roared as lances crossed,
A deadly fight they waged.

Osiris flowed like water,
Seth sharp-fired as flame,
Like a snake his venom pierced,
His fury had no shame.

Through heavens wide the battle raged,
Their blood rained from the sky.
This was a duel that would not end
Till one of them should die.

As storm of battle distant dimmed
At setting of the sun
Osiris lay a vanquished corpse,
Cruel Seth a triumph won.
With knife's keen edge and hatchet sharp,
Osiris he dismembered.
He cast his parts unto the wind
So not to be remembered.
The one exception to this fate,
The phallus he removed.
And fed it to a waiting fish
That lay in Nile's deep ooze.

Among the Nile's dark bulrush,
O'er endless desert sand,
Isis her beloved sought,
In grief she searched the land.
His butchered parts she gathered all,
Except for phallus lost,
She cast death's ashes on her head,
On sorrow's ocean crossed.

Deep in shade of grieving night,
Osiris' parts were lain.
Re-membered was his body,
By Seth his brother slain.
Bitter tears fell on the earth,
Five nights for him she wept.
Despair wreaked havoc on her soul,
A mourning vigil kept.

Strong in silence, fierce in grief,
His body she embalmed.
From Nubian gold new phallus made,
Her song, an ancient psalm
Of rebirth in the underworld,
Of dawn that hope might stir.
Sarcophagus was scented sweet
With frankincense and myrrh.

In depth of night she entered in
The tomb she had created.
Osiris to his life returned
With brother then she mated.
This union did a child conceive,
Seth's vengeance now she feared.
In terror through the delta fled
In marshlands disappeared.

In desert hiding was he born,
Young Horus was his name.
From early years he was fierce-pledged
Their honour to reclaim.
Like a falcon shone he bright,
To manhood fast grew strong.
An army raised 'gainst mighty Seth
—Avenge his father's wrong.

For many years was Egypt split
The deep south from the north.
Till Seth was slain by Horus
A new reign from henceforth.
The line of ancient pharaohs,
In peace ruled through the land.
The rock of civilization
Was now in wisdom's hand.

Awareness like a scarab rolls
Truth's dung across the earth.
From the darkness light does come,
From death there is rebirth.
Man's cruel evil has no bounds,
It leads us to hell's gate.

Her loving wisdom is required
To save us from this fate.

Sweet Isis of the night and day
You guide us birth to death.
These words proclaim your wisdom,
Your truth is on our breath.
Great goddess of the morning,
Love's light across the sky,
You're with all creatures when
they're born,
You love us when we die.

The essence of this precious life,
The seed upon the flower.
The scent within a perfume,
The light that is a star.
The freedom of the wild west wind,
The mist on mountain side,
The thought before you think it,
She knows you from inside.
The sweetness of the desert breeze
You can't grasp in your hands.
She's like the waters of the Nile,
She comes from other lands.

Figure 23. The origins of good and evil in the Egyptian tradition.

The myth of Isis and Osiris is a strong candidate for the most beautiful in the Egyptian pantheon. The story of Osiris' death at the hand of his brother Seth is probably its most dramatic. It was retold across thousands of years of Egyptian history and had numerous versions. They all agree that in the beginning Osiris and Isis, the pharaoh and his sister queen, were happy and in love, rather like a Judaic version of Adam and Eve, a primal couple united in love before the emergence of evil. Both myths, then, locate love as more foundational than evil. Their brother, Seth was malevolently jealous of Osiris. At this point there are different versions, the most coherent and well-known given by Plutarch, a Roman writer of the first century AD, who tells how Seth tricked Osiris to enter a beautiful sarcophagus, then nailed him in and consigned him to the Nile. After being discovered by Isis, Seth found the coffin and then, nothing but thorough, dismembered Osiris. There is another version, found in the Pyramid text (numerous different versions, both in written and visual form, are scattered across Egypt), in which there is a physical battle between the two brothers, at the end of which Osiris is defeated and dismembered by Seth. His body parts are then found by Isis who brings him briefly back to life in order to impregnate her. In all versions she subsequently gives birth to Horus, who later slays Seth and re-establishes the kingdom of peace and good rule, *Maat*, civilization. Osiris leaves earth and is either in the underworld or the starry firmament as a constellation. He embodies the principle of rebirth and justice; he is god of the underworld, judge of the dead. In order to present the different versions the poem above tells the story following the Pyramid texts, while the illustration is of Plutarch's version.

Creative and destructive forces are the underlying structure of good and evil. Osiris and Seth are polar opposites. Moreover, the power of evil appears quite comprehensive with the brutal victory of Seth over Osiris. In the Judaic myth, as described above, the first introduction of psychopathic-type evil is also of one brother towards another—Cain, who also kills his brother Abel. The malevolence of Cain and Seth is based on envy, the intense desire to have what another possesses. Malevolent envy, akin to hatred, is the preparedness to destroy that which one envies. Envy, hatred, and violence occur in the bible, Genesis Chapter Four, immediately after the fall. Likewise, the manifestation of Seth's feelings occurs very early in the story. Clearly, these are regarded by the Egyptians and Jews as primary feelings or forces in the human species, preceding others.

Moreover, in both cases, at least for the modern eye, there is a great deal of obvious psychology—envy between siblings, one brother feeling excluded, the other taking centre stage. The excluded one, in his brother' shadow, grows angrier and more violent until his rage erupts. Such a story is recognisable the world over as a primary and frequent cause of dark feelings in a family. The potential for evil lies embedded in the complex emotions of the human family, where the vulnerable self emerges and is potentially distorted. Both myths posit human evil in malevolent feelings of envy in the family dynamic. However, an underlying division in human consciousness into dark and light, lower and higher potentialities is evident in both the Judaic and Egyptian mythologies.

The Judaic answer to evil in the form of Cain is his banishment. Later transgressions from God's law are counteracted by punishment and the injunction to stay within it. The Egyptian answer is different since there is a feminine principle at work in the form of Isis, who, rescuing Osiris, creates a son who is later to re-establish civilisation. The psychopathic or malevolent evil in mankind does not win out in either the Judaic or Egyptian mythologies but their pathways are different, the Egyptian demonstrating the influence of goddesses and therefore leaning towards a different psychology. There are a number of goddesses in the Egyptian pantheon including Nut, who, far from being confined to the earth, was the goddess of the overarching sky. Again, there is a greater stress on a feminine and positive component of the psyche. Egypt, although a patriarchy, is clearly more linked to the world of the Great Mother. This stands in contrast to the masculine nature of the Abrahamic God with no female companion in the heavens. Nevertheless, the portrayal of evil or psychopathy is even more marked in the Egyptian case since the dismemberment details are far more brutal than those of the Cain and Abel story. Also, in the Egyptian there is no higher God that steps in to solve the problem; Seth and Osiris are already gods and the consequences of their actions are to determine the fate of the human race. However, the idea that there is a beneficent mother who cares for the world, nature, all creatures, and mankind leaves a different imprint on the psyche compared to the Judaic, Christian god who is ultimately transcendent and moral.

CHAPTER SIXTEEN

Evil and the shadow

Satan's Plan

Of all addiction I'm the source
Of lust and also greed,
Destruction I rejoice in,
Desire I turn to need.
Of appetites I take control
I rage against the sacred.
I will not rest until I've seen
This world is full of hatred.

The human heart became my home,
Your mind it is my court.
The body is my playground,
My spies control your thought.
In man's reason put I poison,
Woman's heart is seized by fear.
Children's tongue with lies I planted,
In youths' hands put I a spear.

The animal within you,
The shadow at your back.
I am your carnal appetite,
I'm always painted black.

The psychopath that's in you,
Enhancement that you crave.
I give you so much pleasure,
It drives you to your grave.

The monster in your mind am I,
The canker on the flower.
The source of all confusion,
The sadist with his power.
Destroyer of all precious life,
I kill you in the womb,
The root of every illness,
I'll dance upon your tomb.

By me the light's extinguished,
And hope will always fail.
The psychopathic monster,
I make your mind a jail.
I take your heart and drink your blood,
Your death is my great pleasure.
All life is crushed, sweet joy is doomed,
Destroy I every treasure.

You think you can oppose this force?
By you I am persuaded?
You think you can confront me, sure,
Alone and quite unaided?
You fool, you do not stand a chance
Without some higher help.
My strength's unmatched, my cunning sharp,
I'm lodged inside yourself.

But what are my intentions, pray?
What is my dark plan?
Humans are my instrument,
I own the mind of man.
But this is not enough for me,
My plan has much more worth.
Destroy ALL life is my chief goal,
Annihilate the earth!

You may pray it never happens,
This bitter cup let pass.

Apocalypse is very close,
The sands run through the glass.
My finger's on the button,
Death is finely poised.
Thermonuclear weapons,
They hardly make a noise.

There is no need to lock your door,
No point to make a dash.
Now just you settle down my dear,
It's over in a flash.
The evolution of earth's life
It took four billion years.
Before you know it, all is gone,
There is no time for tears.

The only sound then to be heard,
Supposing you could hear it,
Will be my laughter in the wind,
It's then too late to fear it.
Mankind has been a willing fool,
Earth's life will be quite passed.
My armies rise to other worlds,
The universe is vast.

Figure 24. Evil and the shadow.
To try to fill the state of inner emptiness man is addicted to wealth, pleasure and domination.

Creative and destructive forces, as Hindu and Egyptian mythologies indicated many thousands of years ago, exist as universal principles. They also underpin life on earth and, by implication, the consciousness of humanity. The essence of evil in the psyche is the destruction of the good which is the creative and life-giving in our species. The bad is not the *privatio boni* (the absence of good) of Augustine and the Christian Church but *perditio boni* (the destruction of the good), evil as an active, real force in human beings. Satan means adversary in Hebrew and, therefore, by implication, the Satanic is that which is opposed to the life-giving and creative. The light of consciousness is only matched by its darkness. The view of the human psyche presented here is from a threefold perspective, that of myth, depth psychology, and evolution.

The feeling of alienation or separation from some primal unity, and a consequent longing for a unity with something outside ourselves, is at the root of spiritual endeavour. The awareness of fractures, splits, and divisions in ourselves and a desire to heal these states with a sense of unity is a perennial need. A state of separateness or alienation is therefore the result of the emergence and development of our consciousness, which, by its egoic state, separates out from the immersion in the greater whole and individualises. This state of separation is the first darkness, the shadow of consciousness, and is the root of other negativity in the psyche. It exists at the phylogenetic level of the evolution of consciousness in our race, as well as ontogenetically in the development of consciousness in infants and their separation from immersion in the mother, the great waters, and their subsequent process of individualisation.

From this point of view the Judaic myth makes sense. Consciousness is a separated state and is foundational to the rest of human negativity. The impulse into consciousness is inherent in evolution, and therefore some rupture or structural split occurs in the psyche, that is, between the unconscious and conscious, which leaves mankind in a divided condition. Spiritual and much artistic endeavour is an attempt to overcome this split or "death". It is not surprising that renewal, rebirth, and resurrection motifs abound in the world's religions and arts. They respond to mankind's primal neurosis—separation and the emergence of consciousness. Lucifer in the Judaic myth is, therefore, interpreted here as the impulse to consciousnesses. This is neither evil nor bad but an inevitable opposition to the primal unity. It is differentiation, a separating off, an emergence into "death", a break from the primal unity. It is also the achievement of god-like status with knowledge of good and evil, that is, consciousness. However, its consequences are dramatic since mankind is compelled to answer or compensate for this state of alienation. It also lays the basis for so much that is later problematic in human consciousness. For example, the effort to overcome the emptiness of alienation can produce excessive desire to be filled, to consume, and to compensate for the separated state.

Evil in the human psyche

There has been recently a deep change in our scientific understanding of animal consciousness and of our evolution from primates. Mankind, as an evolved animal, shares instincts, many appetites, passions, and fears with primates and other creatures. Carl Linnaeus, 1707–1778, the great Swedish botanist, said, in his book *Dieta Naturalis*, "One should not vent one's wrath on animals. Theology decrees that man has a soul and that the animals are mere 'aoutomata mechanica', but I believe they would be better advised that animals have a soul and that the difference is of nobility".

Animal intelligence is also a platform for our own intelligence. Primates, especially our nearest relative the chimpanzee, have the capacity for the basic cognition that underlies the human mind, for example, the foundation of language and number. They have the capacity for an awareness of self and can have empathy and altruistic behaviour. They have a degree of autonomy and can also lie, rape, attack, torture, and kill members of their own species. They can intensely bond with their family members and can recognise and be affected by the death of members of their species. So much of their behaviour is fundamental to what is, later in evolution, to be regarded as good and evil in humans.

We have evolved from animals and therefore share our nature with primates, who in their turn evolved from an older mammalian and then reptilian past. Much of human psychology has its distant origin in our animal past. Aggressive and sexual animal instincts are important parts of this inheritance and are so powerful they need to be controlled. Our instinctual life can be a serious threat to social order. Wild and primitive sexual forces are dangerous to social structure and are especially damaging when directed at the helpless and young (see Incest Taboo in Glossary for what Claude Lévi Strauss and Freud said on this topic). Aggressive and even murderous forces needed to be prevented within the social structure but then were channelled outwards where they were most useful in hunting and warrior activities. When civilisation and its laws break down, the aggressive and sexual instincts can surface quickly and there we see marked human evil. The idea that early mankind (both men and women) was essentially benign and peace-loving is, in the view of the author, highly idealistic.

The emergence and development of mankind's consciousness offered a vast arena for the enactment of basic passions, desires, greed, and aggression, which we share with animals. It is through ego consciousness that an elaborated, magnified, and sometimes distorted expression of man's animal appetites occurs. Thus, positive and peaceful parts of this inheritance, for example, nurturing, bonding, maternal, and family instincts become part of our psychology and social behaviour, even transforming (magnifying) into love and selfless devotion. Negative parts, such as the attack and killing instincts, can become the basis for serious psychological disturbance (distortion). The sexual instinct, for example, clearly has the capacity for magnification and distortion. What in an animal is a reproductive impulse, in a human can become obsession and deviation. Addiction is possible in many animals also, but in humans it becomes a dangerous and embedded part of many societies across thousands of years. The "pecking order", understandable in the primate group, becomes distorted and magnified in the human, with distinctions obsessively sought in economic and military systems. These impulses and behaviour patterns have their foundation in our animal nature. There can even be pleasure or satisfaction in evil since human beings have a vast capacity to indulge these appetites, sexual pleasures, desires, and aggressions. Mankind can then become captured by desires and addicted. Many addictions and distortions of the psyche originate in our bodies and in craving for pleasure; some originate in aggression, hatred, psychopathy, and the infliction of pain and destruction on others. Some originate in pursuit of power. Many of these can be found in some degree in other animals especially the pursuit of power, sexuality, and aggression. As humans, besides inheriting these disposition or appetites, we have them magnified through our ego, one of its roles being to serve the passions, to ensure the supply of narcissistic pleasures by which we try to define our existence. The ego is easily caught by the passions and then serves them. Sexuality, in particular, has a range of vice, and again demonstrates the capture of our consciousness and imagination by desire, passion, and the need for gratification. Our primitive instincts are still with us and the majority of humans are dangerously bound into their tribal or nationalist systems, where they identify with their group and are willing to pursue violent and even terminal policies towards other humans.

Badness and evil, perhaps better termed as human negativity, are as real a part of our nature as is love and goodness. Our negative components come through the aggressive, selfish, and destructive components of our animal inheritance as they are transmitted through our psyche, particularly when distorted. In addition, the emergence of human consciousness and the ego leaves us especially vulnerable to anxiety and depression, which easily leads to distortion and aggression. Of all creatures, the human infant is the most helpless for the longest period after birth. The emerging psyche, moreover, is especially vulnerable to deprivation of love and abuse, and this has serious destructive consequences. Negative intra-uterine and birth experiences can have profoundly damaging impacts on the emerging child. We are very easily possessed by feelings of insecurity and abandonment, threats to our status or position in the family, the withdrawal of love, and so on. We have also numerous defences against anxiety. The possibilities for the emergence of human negativity are obvious given our considerable vulnerability, the result of our consciousness, which in infancy has a delicate ego, so sensitive to rebuff, loss of respect, and status. Some of this is also found in primates, who undergo similar emotions in their families systems and groups. However, in the human these dynamics are enormously magnified. Early emotional wounds cause damage to the emerging sense of self and produce defences to protect from further pain. These include withdrawal, denial, splitting, narcissistic compensations, and many more.

The Luciferian and the Satanic are then, by implication, essentially different. Lucifer, the light carrier, is the impulse to consciousness and representative of the separated state of mankind's consciousness—the *fallen* state in Judaic-Christian and Islamic theology. Satan, the adversary, is *perditio boni*, the destroyer of the good, that part of the psyche so capable of becoming distorted and which magnifies the appetitive, selfish, and aggressive forces in our animal inheritance. At its worst it is a psychopathic destruction of the goodness of life and even of life on earth itself—evil. What began as a dragon conquest can end in self and earth annihilation—the fulfilment of the Satanic.

The shadow

Consciousness and the shadow tend to grow in parallel, especially as mankind moved from nature worship to patriarchal religions, which have extensive rules, laws, taboos, prohibition, and sins. The patriarchal religions, in particular by repressing the world of instinct and sexuality, created an enormous, repressed shadow. Thus, a split in the psyche appeared: on the one hand, the ideal, and on the other, the failure or the darkness. Nowhere was this more apparent than in the realm of sexuality in the Abrahamic religions. In the development of Christianity, for example, one observes an increasing anti-sexuality in the early centuries of the church. Original sin was interpreted as a sexual sin of temptation and fall, woman was blamed for being the source of man's sexual desire, and on to her were projected man's fear and his own lust. The Church regime was unremitting and pursued the very thoughts and innermost feelings of its believers. Even a sexual thought or impulse was considered sinful. Origen, a prominent early Church father, actually castrated himself so as to be free of his desires. Much of the writings of the early Church leaders show a titanic struggle with sexual temptation, the essence of the diabolic. The Catholic Church instituted one of the most long-lasting and successful forms of domination in the history of control systems—the confession. Members of the Church were obliged to go to confession regularly and confess their sins—frequently sexual in nature but covering also a wide range of sinful appetites, desires, passions, and aggressions. Having confessed, penitents would be blessed and forgiven their sins. If they were to die in that instant they would go to heaven for eternity. If they died in the night, especially during concupiscence, hell could be their fate. Members of the Church, at one point totalling most of Europe, were completely under the control of this system of thought. The Inquisition (judicial institutions within the Roman Catholic Church in the Middle Ages) combated heresy and could, at one point, investigate, torture, and have killed those they suspected of heresy, sorcery, witchcraft, or even of having views contrary to the doctrines of the Church. The so-called Great Religions have a long shadow.

However, it is not only religions that create the shadow. The whole apparatus of law, social structure, control of behaviour at work, political systems, and so on all shape behaviour and thought. Civilisation *is* the shaping of behaviour and therefore necessarily creates the forbidden and the controlled, which become the darker and repressed sides of the psyche. The shadow, then, is synonymous with repression. It exists at a macro level, as just argued, but it is also very much a micro, individual phenomenon and a most useful working tool in depth psychotherapy. The shadow is the unacknowledged and the repressed in the psyche. Strangely enough, it can also include the "good" and the potential of a human being, which may also be denied and repressed. There can be no proper analysis of the psyche without investigation into this largely unconscious material. The way to work with the shadow in psychotherapy is totally different to the traditional repressive stance of religion. In depth psychotherapy the task is to bring consciousness to bear upon the shadow, to allow it to speak; it often has layers underneath its repressed exterior that can lead to the liberation of the sufferer. Imagine a religion that worked like this. Instead of condemning, repressing, and controlling thoughts and impulses, suppose it brought the light of awareness to the dark material, entered into genuine dialogue with it, and became aware of the layers that lie beneath the shadow, including its healing core. Take sexual phantasy for example, something so prevalent in the human species. With those suffering intense psychological problems sexual phantasy material often has a meaning hidden in its repressed darkness. At its deepest this material has a healing impulse that is unconscious but expressed in the sexual phantasy (Stoller, 1986). Thus, there is frequently a light in the darkness. The challenge is to reach it. The shadow in individual psychology is also the material repressed into the deeper psyche, not only by social structures and ideologies (the superego) but also by automatic defence mechanisms that try to deal with the painful, repressed, or traumatic material in infancy and childhood. The same principles apply here. This material also needs to be brought to consciousness. Inner awareness and deep self-reflection need to approach this painful shadow material and dialogue with it until the hidden core is revealed. For example, underneath murderous anger may lie sorrow and the pain of rejection—the psychology of Seth and Cain who murdered their brothers.

As Jung insisted, the more that shadow material lies undisturbed and unchallenged the greater its power to be projected outwards on to others. This is most notable between groups such as races or nations who easily project their shadow on to "inferior" groups. So intense can this projection be that they may make other groups live out the projection to "prove" to themselves it must be true (technically called "projective identification" in psychoanalysis). Thus, the Nazis in the Second World War could corral and lock the Jews into the Warsaw ghetto, terrorise, starve, murder, and then televise them to prove to their own people how despicable and inferior they were.

The Nazi catastrophe has it psychological roots in the damaged German psyche. Longing for its narcissistic place in the colonial sun, Germany had already in 1914 provoked World War One. The harsh and *humiliating* conditions imposed on it in 1919 by the victors, the economic deterioration of the country in the 1920s, the chaos of its political system, and the serious social deterioration laid the basis for the Nazi party to come to power. Out of disintegration came the grandiose need for reassertion of superiority—the archetypal narcissistic defence. The leader of the Nazi party, Adolph Hitler, was deeply narcissistically damaged with pronounced compensatory mechanisms that included grandiosity, megalomania, and denial. In addition, he was a psychopathological and borderline personality with an extraordinary capacity for hatred, which he projected on to others. A useful and amazingly predictive interpretation of Hitler's psychology—*The Mind of Adolph Hitler*—was written by Walter Langer (1972) in 1943 and used many of the above theories. To say that every country gets the leader it deserves would be a cruel indictment of Germany and of other counties who have suffered such dangerous leaders. But when countries suffer serious structural damage in their political and economic systems, the way becomes open for radical leaders of disturbed personality formation to bluff or manoeuvre themselves into power, and once there it is very difficult to remove them. The consequences for Germany and the whole of Europe were disastrous. If this leader had had access to nuclear weapons (which he missed by a small margin) world history, certainly European history, would have been quite different. Yet this immense and apocalyptic danger is precisely what the world now faces.

CHAPTER SEVENTEEN

The higher self

There is still hope for humankind,
Rich gifts we took from Eden.
"You have a heart, you have a soul,
These lie outside your reason.
They are above your appetite,
Beyond desire and fear.
Face your darkness, see the light,
A voice within you'll hear."

Awareness will awaken you,
Let mind and breathing slow.
Sense a presence in the brow,
Feel its dim light glow.
Still the breath, emotions calm,
Expand now with the light.

You can ask it any question,
You'll find it answers right.
Let it seek out all your wounds,
It has great healing force.
A truth that is impersonal,
It has transcendent source.

Beyond the Tree of Knowledge
Another tree does lie,
Whose roots go deep in earth's dark soil,
Its branches reach the sky.
Enlightenment is promised,
Let light within your soul.
"You will become as gods" he said
Transcendence is our goal.

Figure 25. The higher self.

The emergence of *Homo sapiens* shows a fivefold structure of consciousness: animal inheritance, a complex emotional structure, an ego consciousness, an unconscious, and a higher self. As consciousness evolves and a distinct person comes into existence, a sense of separateness emerges. This, as we have argued, involves the entry into human consciousness of the anxiety of death. The response of the psyche to this death awareness is, first, the emergence of love, and, second, the higher self. Indeed they are closely related and are treated here with a small but distinct difference—no more than that between the fourth (heart) and the sixth (brow) chakra (see Glossary for more information on chakras). For the first 100,000 years of *Homo sapiens'* existence (200–100 thousand years ago), we have little evidence of any "higher" accomplishments. Human populations were at very low levels and our chances of finding intact, archaeological objects are very small. However, from 100,000 years ago there is the first evidence of burials with flowers inside graves. Thus, the anguish of death is met by love, a transcendence of separateness, a desire for the immortal and the deathless.

At the same time as the emergence of death awareness the higher self is triggered into existence and indeed is closely related to love. Our higher self has many attributes, including a capacity for transcendental love, higher intuition, illumination, revelation, music, art, poetry, and advanced forms of symbolic thought that appear revolutionary in evolution. The level and range of our abstract symbolic understanding and expression are extraordinary. Moreover, with the exception of some basic word and even number recognition in chimps and possibly a few other species, there is nothing of their like in the whole animal kingdom. We have suggested above (Part II) that early *Homo sapiens* developed higher awareness (for example, aesthetics) by around 40,000 years ago. The cave paintings referred to show a deep immersion in the world of animals but also a differentiation from the world of nature since now human beings could *depict* them on the Palaeolithic cave walls. The ability to illustrate evocatively, artistically, and accurately a bison or reindeer with a few etched lines upon a mammoth tusk, reindeer bone, or rugged wall is a remarkable symbolic communication and evidence for the development of the abstract thinking, aesthetic sensibility, and high level skill of early *Homo sapiens*. Here we suppose that symbolic thought did originate in the same mental mechanisms that exist in primates but it is a vast leap to the symbolic thought in *Homo sapiens*. The existence of the higher self in humans, we suggest, is a result of the inherent spirit in the cosmos, the *anima mundi*, an intelligence in nature and evolution. It cannot be really explained by a materialist view of evolution, for it has little, if any, survival value. It is grace, primal spirit, embodied in matter.

Human beings, despite a separated, *fallen* state, have been convinced that they are also higher beings, above all other creatures, made in the divine image, and capable of participating again in the primal unity with this divinity. They perceive they have a moral dimension, a capacity for reason, and can raise themselves above carnal instincts; that they have a soul, and even long to transcend death. Also important is the human being's sense of shame, for after the indulging of sexual and aggressive animal instincts the human has a capacity to reflect and feel ashamed and sorrowful. At the centre of our vastly expanded intelligence is a revolutionary capacity for self-awareness, which includes that of deep centres of the psyche which are the core Self. Our self-awareness is convinced of its universality at the same moment as we become aware of death. The higher self gives rise to the existence of principles above narrow self-interest and selfish calculation. It is the evolved master of consciousness, its highest expression. It is the inherent creativity of the human species, its capacity for love, wisdom, and the transcendent.

CHAPTER EIGHTEEN

The experience of love

He guards his arms around his love,
Within them are contained
These precious ones on him depend,
By him they are sustained.
He will labour, he will fight
Until his final breath.
To help them grow towards the light
And not devoured by death.

She will nurture, she will love,
Their sorrows she repairs,
That they may be protected
And never know despair.
She offers all that she can give,
Her essence is the heart.
Her breast is rich and full and strong,
From her they'll never part.

The child will grow within this love,
Such beauty in her soul.
She is lovely, wide and bright,
Cherished to be whole.
On each other they depend,
Each has their position.
The precious gift that they can give
Is love with no condition.

Across one thousand million years
Nature has devised,
That from two loves one more is born,
And reproducing, dies.
It therefore is no secret
From where our love does hail.
It must in nature be inbuilt
Or else this great plan fails.

Figure 26. Love.

Good and evil have their roots in nature and our animal inheritance, in the creative and bountiful as well as in the destructive and selfish. Within nature these are simply forms of survival but in humans they transform into opposites. As well as darkness there is light in our inheritance. There are many manifestations of the higher creative levels of the human psyche but the most powerful and undeniable is that of love. Just as our ego consciousness evolved out of our animal inheritance, so too there are parts of higher emotional functioning, including love, that have roots in our creaturely past—reproductive relations, sexuality, the love of offspring, and family bonds. There is clearly a sense of empathy that can exist among certain primates as well as early humans. There is also love in the sense of sacrificial devotion in many mammals between mother and young. The same applied to early humans.

In species similar to *Homo sapiens* there is evidence of care of the sick, as mentioned above. *Homo neanderthalis*, a parallel species to our own, provides evidence from half a million years ago of such care. At around 100,000 BCE we have evidence of symbolic burial rituals in our own species. We can associate these characteristics with the development of empathy and probably love. However, this is not unique to our genus. Chimpanzees show a capacity to understand that their companions have separate minds; they are capable of grief, and provide other evidence of empathic awareness. In short, love *evolved*. It arises where creaturely bonding meets self-awareness, especially in the human psyche. As consciousness separates out from nature, in mythological terms the fall, it experiences itself as cut off and differentiated, which is, symbolically, a death. It seeks to compensate for this anguish by love and reproduction, that is, by overcoming isolation and alienation with connection and survival. Love is the unconscious attempt to overcome the trauma of death awareness. It is the Garden of Eden, the paradise, the state of wonder and *participation mystique*; it breaks down the defences of the ego; it disregards social convention, crosses boundaries, and defies authority. It proclaims itself as limitless and eternal and therefore transcends death. It opens up a new awareness of everything. It is the essence of being alive because it overcomes death, even if just temporarily—hence the existence of the tragic.

Love, therefore, evolved out of animal inheritance and death awareness of the ego. As human consciousness develops, love expands, beyond its immediate family identification, outwards to others, to the world, to the universe, and inwards to an awareness of love within the self. Love can become a principle of all, the highest reality. Love redeems fallen mankind from separateness and the futility of vice. Ice-age art of around 25,000 years ago shows figurines that are popularly known as Venuses. Undoubtedly, they demonstrate man's preoccupation with the female body, sexuality, and reproduction (their Venus quality). They also demonstrate his love for woman because it is through sexuality that this love is realised and then deepened through children—the means by which man and woman become more whole. However, the Goddess of Laussel bass relief (see Part II), also of a naked woman, is 20,000 years old and declares a symbol in her right hand which is held up clearly for the viewer to see. It is a horn of cornucopia, the rebirth of the waning and waxing moon with thirteen etches upon it. These refer, surely, to the lunar and possibly menstrual cycles. Moon, month, and menstrual have the same etymological root: Latin *mensis* (month), and Greek *men/mene* (month/moon). It can be inferred that here is an awareness of an identification between the human and lunar cycles. Mankind is part of the greater whole, which is linked to the feminine, a universal principle underlying all of nature and human kind, an overarching divine force that permeates all "creation". Thus, an awareness and love of all creation is constellated in the emergence and development of our consciousness.

All religions have stressed the transcendental value and healing impact of love. It opposes the negativity of violence, aggression, and evil and redeems the human from the darkness of his animal inheritance. In the Christian religion love has been exalted as its supreme value. Paul in his famous letter to the Corinthians writes …

> If I speak with the tongues of men, and of angels, and have not love, I am become as sounding brass … And if I should have prophecy and should know all mysteries, and all knowledge, and if I should have all faith, so that I could remove mountains, and have not love, I am nothing … And now these three remain: faith, hope and love. But the greatest of these is love.
>
> (I Corinthians 13:1–13. New Testament Bible)

The great religions have insisted on the foundations of love in the human psyche as its most redeeming feature. Love has existed from the beginnings of our species in earthly love of mother and child, man and woman, and within the family. This later co-universalised with our consciousness to become a love of nature, the world, and beyond. The early period of the Great Mother shows evidence in the form of artefacts (some mentioned above) of this process, demonstrating a love and fascination of the world and its creatures, and an awareness of an immense creative force underlying nature and of the human being as part of it. Unless we love the earth like our own mother we are likely to destroy her; unless we find love within ourselves we are likely to destroy each other.

PART V

THE ENLIGHTENMENT AND CAPITALIST PROJECT

The history of consciousness has been simplified in three stages: first, the immersion in nature worship, which is broadly the period from 40,000 to around 3,000 BCE; second, the emergence of patriarchal religions, which in the Near East and the West were focused on a single transcendent God—a period stretching from around 3000 BCE to *circa* 1600 CE; third, and now to be presented, the Enlightenment and the capitalist project, the age of materialism and science in which a new consciousness emerges, eventually dispensing with gods and myths. Each of these are vast periods of history with numerous sub-periods and developments. Nevertheless, this book concentrates only on the broad aspects of this development.

The age of religions was challenged in Europe by the renewal of free thinking and science from around the seventeenth century onwards—the Enlightenment project. The new system that crystallised out of the revolutions and transformations that were to follow was capitalism. Its inner motor was technological transformation. It is the most creative yet destructive economic system in history.

Chapter Nineteen examines the source of the achievements of capitalism, concentrating on the nature of its economic system and what distinguishes it from other economic formations: its dynamism; its relationship to the State; its flexibility; and its psychology. Transformations in consciousness and especially religious ideologies were necessary for its birth in the Protestant countries of Northern Europe and America. Later it cast off all forms of religious belief, creating a new type of consciousness in humanity.

Chapter Twenty presents capitalism as crisis. While accomplishing immense advances in material production and wealth creation capitalism is prone to serious crises. In particular, the money and banking system become semi-autonomous and seriously endanger the system. In addition, capitalism has a tendency to undermine its supposed competitive base by the creation of cartels and monopolies. It also is very dependent on the State, especially in crisis; it creates serious inequalities of wealth; and, of especial importance, it leads to highly destructive ecological and military crises that threaten our survival on the planet.

Chapter Twenty-one tackles the central question: How has consciousness changed with capitalism? It provides answers at many levels, including; the removal from nature; the diminishing or disappearance of religious ways of thinking; a greater materialism; a more rational and economic viewpoint; greater individualism, a consumerist attitude, greater specialisation, increased education, and greater expectation of freedom. It ends with a consideration of *informational capitalism*, the contemporary situation where consciousness is beginning to fuse with digital systems and artificial intelligence, producing yet another profound shift of consciousness itself.

Chapter Twenty-two, "Death potential in consciousness", presents the shadow of the capitalist and Enlightenment project by which it destroys the earth with economic calculus, greed, destructiveness, and malignant impulses for self-aggrandisement. Existential threat to our species is now potentialised.

INTRODUCTION

The scientific revolution and capitalism

The age of patriarchal religions, which in one form or other dominated the consciousness of humanity for thousands of years, was challenged in Europe from the seventeenth century onwards. A growing belief in the findings of science, a series of political revolutions that freed millions from the semi-enslavement of feudal systems, and the birth of the most productive economic system in world history were a series of Promethean hammer blows that shattered the old paradigms and forged a new order out of the fiery transformations of the centuries that followed. It was also a revolution in human consciousness, which was no longer in a cosmological prison where a scientist such as Galileo could be threatened with torture for arguing that the earth goes around the sun, but, instead, was a place where enlightened enquiry was free to fly to what height it dared. Britain, central to the scientific and industrial revolutions, was different from Ancient Greece, which, for a brief period, had some of the most astounding free thinkers, including those of science, the world had ever seen, for it managed to develop its freedoms of the market and democracy, while in Greece these were to perish. Above all, the scientific revolution was to be linked with an economic system that could turn inventions to profit and technologies to world domination. The Greek and also Roman systems, despite democratic components, were founded on slavery, a military system, and, for some periods, a dictatorship. Such economies, despite enormous achievements and progress, did not possess the essential freedoms for capitalism to develop.

In the field of cosmology the European medieval Catholic Church was based on a literal reading of Genesis and an acceptance of ancient Roman cosmology (Ptolemy). However, with the Enlightenment, in those few countries that could tolerate free thought, new knowledge was empirical and subject to testing. The theory of planetary motion around the sun, like thousands of other scientific hypotheses, can be tested and proven. With this revolution in consciousness, understanding the world was now without reference to a God and was reconstructed according

Figure 27. The achievements of capitalism.

to the laws of physics, chemistry, biology, and mathematics. This was the first system of thinking that was not mythological but was pragmatic, empirical, and deductive. A series of theoretical discoveries, including that of evolution, had an enormous impact on our view of human nature and the universe. Immense sources of energy, such as those of coal, electricity, gas, oil, and nuclear energy transformed human existence and its consciousness. New transport systems revolutionised industrialising economies. The emerging social and economic structures were revolutionary in their impact.

The economic system is the altar at which mankind now worships; it is the central reference point, the supraordinate authority and the determiner of wealth or poverty; it determines even the moral values of the population. The end result of the materialist philosophical revolution, however, is a belief in a soulless universe. The market is the new god—except it is empty of inner life. Some will say that mankind is better off without oppressive clerical control; that it is better to live in the pain and isolation of freedom rather than the false security of misguided, totalitarian religions. Yet, what ethic is to guide humanity when it is now capable of destroying its own species and life on this earth? Capitalism, of all the economic systems known to mankind, is the most creative and destructive. Where is its guide? Does it have any principles outside of itself to orientate it? Or is it completely self-referential? Capitalism has raised to unprecedented heights the standard of living of increasing parts of the world's expanding population. How has it done this? Is the capitalist system fundamentally flawed? And how is consciousness part of this process? Were changes in consciousness and belief required for the birth of this revolutionary economic system? Has the consciousness of modern man under capitalism changed? It is often debated whether capitalism will be replaced but the realistic question is whether humanity will avoid self-destruction with the instruments that capitalism and the Enlightenment project has created.

CHAPTER NINETEEN

The source of the achievements of capitalism

Capitalism is the most creative and the most destructive economic system in mankind's history. First, we examine the source of its creativity.

1. **Its economic mechanisms** are, on the whole, highly efficient and generate enormous wealth. This is a result of:

    a. the extensive use of a *price mechanism* determined by supply and demand, forming an automatic distribution system (Adam Smith's "invisible hand") for investment, production, and consumption;
    b. a competitive *system* that deeply influences price, quality, and new product creation;
    c. a *circulatory reinvestment process* whereby technologies and labour are harnessed to create products, sold for profit, and reinvested back in production—the key to the growth process. Other systems have generated surplus but the competitive process of capitalism *obliges* firms to reinvest, or they fail in the competitive race.

2. **Its dynamism** produces:

    a. *Intense waves of technological transformation*, typically beginning with a series of central inventions and diversifying into numerous innovations providing new profit opportunities, employment, products, and firms. These have revolutionary impact;
    b. *Social transformation* of many types, for example, urbanisation explodes with capitalism, since cities are economic engines possessing tremendous advantages of cost savings and productivity propelling economic activity, generating jobs and profit opportunities;
    c. *Global expansion*. Capitalism seeks trade, raw materials, labour, and markets across the globe. It developed in pulses of transformation around the earth and became the world's

dominant economic system. Capital seeks global expression and brings the whole world into its embrace. Financial globalisation accompanies or rapidly follows the spread of trade to all corners of the globe.

3. **Its relationship to the State**—although the State was meant to be minimalist in the new capitalist system, in fact its power has grown and the amount of social capital (infrastructure, utilities, education, health, and so on) in its hands increased enormously. The State did not decrease its power but changed its support for the emerging capitalism instead of for the system that historically preceded it. The strength of capitalism lay in its power to "capture" the State.
4. **Its flexibility**—the different varieties of capitalism across the globe, from the US (free market) to Sweden (social democratic) as well as its ability to combine with other systems (e.g., communism in China) is impressive. Even within the same country there is considerable flexibility of capitalism across time, for example, from the Keynesian semi-socialist UK of the 1960s to the free enterprise system of the 1990s. In addition, US and UK policy response to their two largest crises of 1929 and 2008 shows adaptation and policy change. In brief, capitalism evolves and changes very quickly, and its relationship to the State has proved flexible to the most serious crises.
5. **Its psychology is based upon**:
    a. *Self-interest*. Capitalism has the immense advantage that it taps into mankind's most basic psychology. Other economic formations, such as feudalism or slavery, are based on psychological principles that are unproductive. The psychology of private gain is built into human nature with its unconscious infantile longing, hunger, and greed.
    b. *Private wealth and property*. The retention of the wealth in private hands generated by this system is vital, otherwise the incentive to engage in productive efforts is pointless. Capitalism, therefore, gives the assurance that this wealth is protected.
    c. *Ideological justification*. Capitalism, despite imperfections, claims equilibrium at its centre, a market mechanism that works efficiently with minimum state interference, when laws are obeyed and the State provides a platform (infrastructure, education, police, defence, etc.) for it to function. It justifies itself by providing greater wealth for a greater number of people than any other system and equates wealth with happiness. In addition, it provides incomparably more freedoms, including political and individual, than any other system.
    d. *A change in consciousness*. Capitalism requires a change in mentality, attitude, and belief to emerge historically and, in turn, has profoundly changed human consciousness and continues to do so. Its ability to change consciousness is crucial to its success.

CHAPTER TWENTY

Capitalism as crisis

Icarus

Bold Icarus with father lay,
In prison quite forgot.
At pleasure of King Minos,
Condemned were they to rot.
Escape did not seem possible,
Confined by triple walls.
On dizzy cliffs the prison perched,
Grim death would follow fall.

But Daedelus his father
Would not accept defeat.
He was the master craftsman,
Who felt that he could cheat
These walls and chains and fearsome cliffs,
To cunning would succumb,
If only he could form a plan,
From Minos they would run.

As he watched through prison's bars,
The free-birds fall and rise.
His restless mind conceived a scheme
—Escape into the skies.
Light feathered wings he did construct,
Some wax then used as glue,
He made a harness out of rope,
From cliffs at dawn they flew!
With only this proviso,
He cautioned to his son:
"Fly not too high, the wax will melt
On rising near the sun."

Into the blue empyrean,
They soared like joyful birds.
But with the prison walls now gone,
The son forgot those words.
In wild ecstatic flight he rose,
Below his father saw,
The feathers melt, the wings collapse,
Down to the earth he falls.

And so it is with *capital*,
It longs for its escape
From prisons of stagnation,
Fresh schemes it then creates.
To heights it is addicted,
Forgets the recent past,
Denies its limitations,
This time the boom will last.

Into dizzy heights it soars,
Self-interest turns to greed.
What was reason now goes mad,
The vultures come to feed.
But at the height the bubble cracks,
The boom turns into bust.
It goes the way that all flesh goes,
Returning into dust.

Those of us who rise so high
With caution cast to wind,
Forgetting roots, disdain the rest,
Who think we've never sinned.
Those of us who think we're gods
And masters of our fate,
Like Icarus our wings may melt
On nearing heaven's gate.

Figure 28. Icarus.

The destructiveness of capitalism is now examined:

a. *The price mechanism and invisible hand* do not prevent periodic financial crisis, which follow exceptional booms. At the start of these cycles investment capital pours into new profit opportunities; the banking system inflates the boom creating a speculative, over-financed bubble typically turning into mania. A tipping point is reached, collapse is triggered, prices of stocks and assets connected to the boom decrease, and profits turn to losses. From inflation to depression—the psychological and economic vocabulary are interchangeable.
b. *Money gains a semi-independent existence* since banks are sources of money creation. The control by central banks of their own banking system has usually been insufficient in expansionary periods of capitalism. Banks play a major part in augmenting every boom by credit creation and they are at the root of all major financial collapses. Intertwined with the official banking system lies an enormous financial area of speculation and investment. The creation of vast, financial speculative bubbles is like Frankenstein's monster, an apparently brilliant creation but with a life of its own, towering over the real world of production and exchange, threatening to destroy it.
c. Capitalism, despite its competitive ideals tends to produce *cartels and monopolies*. When industries start their life cycle with small firms, there is frequently an impulse towards large-scale firms emerging, which produce at much lower average cost and at larger volume scales. Some industries and trades, however, will stay dominated by small and micro suppliers since they do not possess economies of scale by which cost reductions are generated at higher-volume levels. This leads, in some industries, to a natural development of oligopolies, cartels, and monopolies. Thus, competitive, free-market capitalism undermines itself and produces uncompetitive market structures. The dangers of this are evident in the financial system, with increasing levels of concentration and dominance. The top three banks in the UK, for example, in 2015 owned assets five times the size of the UK GDP. (Haldane, 2010)
d. Capitalism, in reality, is allied to and dependent on the State. Although this is, as previously indicated, a strength, at the same time it illustrates a weakness of the economic system—it is crucially dependent on the State and without it could not function. Poor or mistaken policies, for example, can lead very rapidly to an economy's ruin.
e. *Capitalism and world domination.* Capitalism replaces all previous economic systems which are far less productive. It cannot be confined to one area, region, or country. Thus, fear and desire (or greed) are the psychological drivers of the system, which, as it expands, eliminates other less efficient economic formations. Native people and their ways of life are destroyed, feudal systems are replaced, and agrarian ways of life disappear. As capitalism develops it tends to replace even previous stages of its own system. Thus, mercantilist capitalism is replaced by industrial capitalism, which, in turn, is replaced by post-industrial capitalism (service-sector dominated economies).
f. *Capitalism and inequality.* To impose equality of income and wealth destroys incentive and competition. Capitalism depends on incentives for personal gain and advancement. Without this the economy cannot function, technological progress disappears, and wealth creation dries up. Inequality arises from many sources and a certain degree of inequality is inevitable in every system, especially in capitalism. However, that does not excuse the gross inequalities

that occur as capitalism leans towards a free-market philosophy. There is no doubt that this can be mitigated by intelligent and prudent redistributions through taxation, welfare states, public goods, and the like. It is getting the balance correct for an individual country that is tremendously difficult.

g. *Capitalism—destruction and extinction*. Many of the technologies of capitalism have a destructive impact on the planet and its animal life. Mankind has always exploited the resources of the world but capitalism is most adept at doing this because of the immense development of these technologies.

From Paradise to Destruction

From Eden cast in fallen state,
To world of death condemned,
Both Eve and Adam tears did shed,
This paradise must end.
Banished into endless toil,
Out of primal grace,
The shadow within consciousness,
Then gripped the human race.
Economic systems rise,
But never calm our fear.
Towards the gates of death we go,
If you have ears, then hear.

Figure 29. From paradise to destruction.

CHAPTER TWENTY-ONE

How has consciousness changed with capitalism?

Capitalism, like all economic activity, is an attempt to overcome the insecurity of existence and the anxiety of death with material production and increased consumption. In this it has outpaced, by a long distance, all other economic formations. Neither is there an alternative system remotely in view that could replace its prodigious accomplishments. However, as a consequence, enormous destructive impacts are inflicted, consciously or unconsciously, on the planet as well as on many of its species. Mankind not only uses nature but thinks he is its master. Technology is the concrete embodiment of mankind's ideas and experiments as they extract "value" from the world. These, in turn, change consciousness, belief, confidence, and self-identity. Consciousness and its products, especially technologies, are inextricably interdependent from the beginning of our species. This way of looking at consciousness and its creations, as a mutually interactive *system*, is the methodology of this chapter. It contrasts, on the one hand, with the hard materialism of a Marxist that views consciousness and culture as the superstructure determined by the economic base—the mode of production of any particular system. On the other hand, it differs from the idealist position that views society, or even the world, as being determined by ideas. The *systemic* method views these opposites as mutually determining one another.

Changes of consciousness and of technologies mutually influence one another as interacting parts of an economic system. Changes in material and social conditions go hand in hand with changes in consciousness, value systems, and even moral beliefs. Thus, consciousnesses as well as economic and material conditions co-evolve rather than one necessarily preceding the other.

As the Protestant Reformation gathered force in Northern Europe it was precisely the Protestant countries, England, Holland, and Northern Germany, where the birth and development of capitalism was most pronounced. A change in consciousness was made possible by

Protestantism, with its break from the Catholic mentality that was essentially anti-capitalistic. Protestantism, especially Calvinism, was particularly suited to the "spirit" of capitalism. By capitalist "spirit" Weber meant *ethic*, or the prevailing beliefs, attitudes, and mentalities necessary for the development of this economic formation, for example, individualism, rationalism, a calculating mind, economic vocation, and a sense of destiny. Money-making and usury were no longer pejorative activities, this earthly life no more a vale of tears; the entrepreneur had a religious calling to produce in this world and to provide employment. His riches were a sign of carrying out God's will rather than of sins. Protestantism tended to favour saving, thrift, and investment, "virtues" dear to early capitalism. Thus, the foundations of a change of consciousness were laid down in the great religious turmoil of the fifteenth to the seventeenth centuries and the growth of Protestantism, as Weber (2003) has clearly shown. The development of industrial capitalism was the most powerful of the developments of capitalism in general. The transformation of town, countryside, and their populations was revolutionary. The productivity gains of the new technologies and factories were extraordinary and provided vast profits.

Capitalism has been the most inventive and revolutionary economic system in the history of mankind. Technologies are typically developed by individuals or firms and then spread to the rest of the population. In so doing they transform the consciousness of those that adopt them. While individuals and firms in the industrial revolution were the creators of inventions and innovations, the impact of these on the mass of the expanding population was enormous. Thousands of innovations stemmed from these revolutionary inventions, such as steam, electricity, or informational technologies. Capitalism, allied to the scientific revolution of the Enlightenment, transformed economic, social, and political structures. This altered the consciousness of the populations in the capitalist system at every level. While capitalism, science, and technology obviously are products of human consciousness, at the same time they very much shape it. Economic systems and their technologies substantially change the social relationships of production and force changes in mentality and belief. Capitalism has been one of the major forces changing the nature of consciousness. We now specify some of these changes.

The removal from nature. All technologies, social structures, and economic systems separate mankind from nature. Capitalism, however, has done this more radically than any other previous formation. To choose one example, the forces of urbanisation, with the mass of the labour force working in factories or offices, with only a few per cent of the labour force working in agriculture, has now become the norm for advanced capitalist countries. The rest of the world follows the trend. Capitalism has brought modernisation at a revolutionary pace and no country can resist its enormous temptations.

A material view of the world. Capitalism is a supremely materialist system. The combination of science and wealth convinces those in advanced economies that a material and scientific view of the world is correct. The superstitions of the past are rapidly abandoned. The knowledge of evolution, medicine, and science leads to a conviction that all previous systems of thought belong in the dark ages. Capitalism has managed to take advantage of the advances of the Enlightenment while disposing of religious consciousness, even the Protestantism that facilitated its development in the West.

The increasingly rational and economic viewpoint. Capitalism was made possible by changes in religious consciousness, which became less Catholic and more Protestant. This new consciousness, from the beginning, even in Calvinist and Puritan format, was more rational and inclined to the economic view. The workplace became dominated by technology and science which emphasised the importance of reason and calculation. We are thus increasingly removed from the world of nature, instincts, and emotions and subject to the mindset required by current and profitable technologies. Competition forces the pressure. We must not only serve the machine, but must think like it. In addition, our societies are dominated by the evolving technologies that transform our landscape, our relationship to nature and to other humans. Even marriage, family relationships, the training of children, and the formation of consciousness of the infant are affected at a profound level by its forces.

The abandonment of religious outlook. While certain types of religious outlook, such as Protestantism, favour capitalism, the prevailing temperament of the system, being allied to modern science, is anti-spiritual and religious. This becomes more pronounced as the Enlightenment project proceeds. However, it leaves mankind empty or "disenchanted" to use Max Weber's expression (see Glossary). Carl Jung (2001) characterised the contemporary condition as "modern man in search of a soul" (the title of one of his better-known books and also one of the leitmotifs of his life's work). Since capitalism destroys all previous religions it empties the psyche of prior religious conceptions. Paradoxically, this clearing of the ground of past superstitions and exhausted mythologies sets the scene for the potential emergence in the twenty-first century of a new spiritual consciousness that may reawaken when the materialist project of the Enlightenment reaches its crisis.

More individualistic. Capitalism breaks down the extended family system, the natural container for identity formation for millennia. The nuclear family system has become prevalent in advanced capitalist economies since the extended family is no longer an economically viable structure. Capitalism "requires" immense flexibility and demands total compliance to its evolving requirements and technologies—even with the nature of family structure. Capitalism produces more individualism but less *individuation*. The market system does not encourage more evolved individuals but rather that they subordinate their personal needs to the business. It demands psychological and collective conformity to market values. In capitalism, people live and work in vast masses. Dissociation, disenchantment, separateness become the norm. Modern man is individualised or atomised in the sense of being more separated from the extended family, its traditions, and his ancestors but he is collectivised in his mentality, attitudes, and beliefs. The intense individualism of the system was prefigured in the emerging Protestantism of the sixteenth and seventeenth centuries, with its stress on the conscience of individuals and direct personal relationship to God. A guilt-ridden, work-obsessed, individualised (separated off) worker is more suited to the capitalist system. The salvatory materialism of the entrepreneur was also an ideal psychology for early capitalism. Durkheim (1951), despite his emphasis on the social, stressed the role of individualism in modern society, suggesting that the individual has become sacred. This modern form of the collective conscience he called the "cult of the individual".

An economic view of societal relationships. As population expands and the division of labour increases, the binding force of societies is less that of religion, class, clan, family systems, national identity, or the old system of beliefs, but increasingly one based on economic interrelationships. The old system of "collective consciousness" (Durkheim's term), of religion, beliefs, and culture is replaced by a new type of solidarity where people are bound together economically by the division of labour of the modern economy—a move from mechanical to organic solidarity (Durkheim, 1984).

A legalistic view of relationships. Civilisation and law are developed together—if one breaks down so does the other. Adam Smith summarised … "If justice is removed … the immense fabric of human society … must in a moment crumble into atoms" (Smith, 2010, p. 86). Capitalism is saturated in law. Previous social structures, of course, also had law but, as explained by Durkheim, they had, also, considerable influence from authority, charisma, tradition, and religion. Under capitalism it is legal relations upon which the nexus of society is based, especially for its great number of exchanges of labour, goods, services, and money, which require an extensive system of law and contract to legalise them.

Specialisation but fragmentation of knowledge. Capitalism replaces the greater self-sufficiency typical of premodern systems of agrarian land holdings with the interconnected market dependency of the modern economy. Increased division of labour is a central motor of capitalism's productivity (Smith, 2003, ch.1). Workers and firms, the basic units of the economy, are ever more specialised. Profit is made from the productivity gains of increasing specialisation. Immense knowledge is contained in the system as a whole, but individual workers and firms are specialised in only a tiny fragment of it. Individuals rarely have knowledge of how the product is made as a whole. For Marx, mankind is alienated from the products it creates because the result of its labour is "taken from" the worker by the capitalist and sold. Jean-Baptiste Say, on reading Adam Smith, commented more existentially: "to have never done any thing but make the eighteenth part of a pin is a sorry account for a human being to give of his existence" (Say, 1803). Capitalism with its intense division of labour produces a more specialised but narrower consciousness, dependent on, but largely ignorant of, the nature of the products and services it creates. The human serves the machine.

Money relationships are dominant—the nexus of human relationship increasingly becomes based on money. A money economy operating through the price system is the platform for wealth creation and also for freedom. The oppressive rights of slavery, the feudal requirements of peasant and serfs, the demands to stay within the same locality, and hundreds of other restrictions are lifted by the money economy, which requires far greater mobility of all factors of production—including human beings. Individuals have economic meaning in so far as they understand and follow the signals of the market. On the one hand, this gives a great deal of freedom while, on the other, it reduces an individual's identity to an economic value.

Greater education. Capitalism requires increased education for its populations, distinguishing it from all previous systems, which only required education for certain strata of society (priests and bureaucracy). Other systems had little interest in educating the masses—quite often the contrary. However, capitalist countries are in competition with one another and the quality of human capital (the education and skill of the workforce) is a vital contribution to productivity and therefore the wealth of a nation. Consequently, the average citizen of a capitalist country is far more cognitively educated than in any other system. Indeed, this process continues during the various stages of capitalism, with more education in its late, compared to early, periods.

Wealth creation and enjoyment. Contrary to Marx's prediction of the growing proletariat and its impoverishment, there has generally been a rising tide of wealth upon which many have risen. Growing wealth creates new consciousness, a sense of mastery, entitlement, happiness, as well as a belief that what one is doing is justified. Consciousness and its value framework thus become "captured" by the success of the system and the value and morals of capitalism become dominant. However, this is periodically shattered by crises that come from the clear sky of prosperity and devastate the economy, such as the depression of 1929 and the financial paralysis of 2008. Thus, periods of wealth, boom, and inflationary confidence are punctuated by slump and depression. Excessive risk-taking, debt, acquisitiveness, and consumerism create an unstable and exaggerated psychology. However, this is not to deny that the increasing wealth provided by this system has considerably increased happiness and relieved the poverty, misery, early death, and poor health that has typified humanity for much of its previous existence.

Consumerism. A great deal of the immense technological and productive forces of capitalism translate into consumption—the end goal of the system. In 2013 almost seventy per cent of US GDP consisted of personal consumption. In UK it approached sixty-six per cent. This was not always the case since in early stages of the system there was more emphasis on thrift, savings, and investment. As the system moves to maturity/decadence there is more emphasis on consumption. China, still fresh on the capitalist scene, has personal consumption levels of forty-eight per cent of GDP in 2012. This figure is rising fast as China "matures". Modern capitalist men and women are, then, immense consumers and this has profoundly influenced their consciousness, their apparent sense of mastery, entitlement, arrogance, and destructiveness.

Property ownership. Individual property rights and ownership lie at the core of any notion that capitalism is a participatory system. To take just one example, home ownership is the single biggest investment that most individuals make. In the UK, by 1975 half its households were owner-occupiers. By 2003 it was seventy per cent. Between 2003 and 2014 UK property ownership declined due to the exceptionally high prices of UK housing—an example of how the inflation of credit booms can impoverish whole sections of any population no longer able to afford housing of its own. However, it can be safely said that a comparative feature of later capitalism is that higher percentages of the population are generally property owners, and therefore participatory, compared to in any other system. Property ownership changes consciousness, creating responsibility, a disposition to long-term care, an investment in stability and community, an awareness of prices and value, and a conservative frame of mind. Investing in property entails also investing emotionally in neighbourhood, country, and system.

Technological reliance. Technology shapes and deeply effects those who use it. Capitalism is the most intensive technological economic system that has ever existed. There is incessant technological competition, driven by the search for profits that when reinvested encourage more technological growth. While the period of industrial capitalism facilitated a more technological mindset in the working classes, under late capitalism this largely disappears, as computerisation, artificial intelligence, and intense specialisation leave the mass of population ignorant about the real workings of even elementary technology. At the same time, there is greater technological reliance in the general population. Technology and the economic and military system, though created by the knowledge of the human race, very soon stand over and dominate it, an external projection of consciousness, a reification that in turn shapes consciousness and social relationships.

Greater freedom. Karl Marx insisted that workers in the capitalist system were not free, but obliged to work under exploitative conditions because they did not own the means of production, which were in the hands of the capitalist class. Nevertheless, the freedoms enjoyed by the mass of the population within capitalist systems (especially those with strong democracies) are infinitely greater than within any previous or alternative systems (apart from hunter-gatherers). These are not just economic freedoms but include those of education, leisure, culture, occupation, lifestyle choice, travel, religion, political systems and many more—this is especially the case for the later capitalist stages in advanced economies. These freedoms have become central to the postmodern discourse in which all aspects of tradition, be they premodern or modern, have been disposed of in post-modernity or late capitalism. The modern that is disposed of includes even many of the paradigms of the Enlightenment project, including those of science and class structure (Giddens, 1991). Objective truth no longer exists and what is valid is self-created, or created within a culture—these are self-referential systems of meaning. Morals, beliefs, attitudes are no longer determined by an outside authority, such as church, class, tradition, or science, for example, but are constructed in the evolving pluralistic and self-referential space of culture, media, political correctness, and individual desire.

This new open space, then, does not have tradition to fill it. The inner world of the individual, such as moral belief, either no longer exists or is minimal or politically determined and is not capable of contending with a crisis; it is no longer determined with reference to religion or the guidelines of the past. As Durkheim (1984) noted, these traditional forms of meaning have been replaced in capitalism by a system of economic interconnectedness—it is the division of labour that is the glue that binds millions together. One's economic place in society gives one meaning. As long as there is economic growth and prosperity then it is easy to forget the inner world, the individual's need for meaning and for a place in the great scheme of things. Outer wealth is paralleled by inner poverty. However, when the economic crisis comes, when millions are thrown into unemployment, financial systems collapse, governments prove corrupt and inept, the authority of the Church collapses, and when tradition offers no guidance these individuals are exposed, not just to economic deprivation but to meaninglessness. Thus, freedom turns to emptiness as economic promise fades.

Informational capitalism is the term the author prefers for the latest stage of the capitalist system since it implies not only the immense technological change of the information revolution but also changes in mentality and of consciousness itself. The age of information technology is the latest and possibly the most profound shift in the consciousness of humanity, which is becoming fused with digital and virtual realities. Many of the points mentioned above (removal from nature, technological rationalism, and so on) become more intensified. The nuclear family becomes almost defunct, marriage and reproduction no longer meaningful or required, and even labour itself, that which previously gave meaning and purpose, is set to become more obsolete, a rarity, as a post-human condition becomes now possible with the increasing advance and eventual dominance of technologies in the form of super-artificial intelligence. Something radically new is occurring in consciousness—the hyperreal becomes the new reality. Hyperreality is a term in postmodern philosophy indicating the difficulty of distinguishing reality from a simulation of reality, particularly in technologically dominated societies. The real and the fictional become impossible to separate, digital and psychical reality co-mingle, human and artificial intelligence fuse (Baudrillard, 1994).

We began this book with mankind immersed in the world of nature—a *participation mystique*. We now glimpse postmodern capitalism, where the emerging consciousness of a new age may be described as a *participation virtuelle*—an immersion, a fusion of our consciousness with digital technologies and, shortly, with artificial intelligence.

CHAPTER TWENTY-TWO

Death potential in consciousness

Mankind is full of conflict,
Forever passion's slave,
Swayed by anger or by fear
We never cease to crave.
The animal within us
It suffocates our heart.
We have to feed it every day,
It might tear us apart.

Thinking is our special gift,
Designed to take control.
Scientific argument
Says reason is our goal.
In spite of best endeavours
Of law, of church and State,
The savage that's inside us all
So quickly turns to hate.

If this is all that humans have,
Just appetite and reason,
We won't be here for very long
Beyond the nuclear season.
The rivalry of nation states
Will have had its day.
Sunless winters will ensure
Earth's life will soon decay.

A trauma waits the human race,
The sands are running fast.
The species will reduce its size,
Our world it will not last.
Extinction though we may escape,
But horror is at hand.
Survivors shall a dark age face,
Death will stalk the land.

What then? Perhaps we start anew,
Fresh principles required.
Foundations strong must then be built,
Or time will have expired.
There will be myths of some great past,
When fire and water reigned.
When humans near destroyed themselves,
Their shadow uncontained.

These are the times we live in,
Our fate is self-imposed.
We're clearly so unconscious,
Our dangerous shadow grows.
Unless we readjust our aims
From short term finite goals,
We're damned within our appetites,
We're doomed without our souls.

This precious earth we cannot save
Only with the mind.
We limit our intelligence
When soul is left behind.
We need a greater vision,
New leaders are required.
Its economic greed and power
By which we are inspired.
There's little time to change this now,
We've plundered all the earth.
See our darkness, know our fate,
Through death seek our rebirth.

The planet is our paradise,
So much has been destroyed.
Revelling in aggression still,
The balance's finely poised.
The sower casts the seed far wide,
The cosmos has a soul.
This seed is planted in our breast,
It's there to make us whole.

Figure 30. "Now I am become death, the destroyer of worlds."

Truthful words are not pleasant,
Pleasant words are not trustworthy.

—*Tao Te Ching*, Chapter 81

In the Hebrew bible when Adam and Eve are banished from the Garden of Eden for taking the fruit of the Tree of Knowledge (the birth of consciousness) there is a fear that they could now also take the fruit of the Tree of Life in the centre of the Garden, gain immortality, and become as God. But, following this mythological way of thinking, we suggest that this cannot happen until death is overcome in the *fallen* state. Only when mankind has evolved into its differentiated, individualised consciousness, separated from the totality, banished from the Garden, do we face our fallen nature—our vices and appetites. Consciousness and its enormous powers are a temptation to achieve dominance over the earth, its resources, and its life, which leads to the creation of vast economic systems for the accumulation of wealth and the invention of weapons. However, these systems provide not only material abundance but have the present capacity to destroy life on earth—certainly our species. Human consciousness can self-destruct, constituting not a death instinct but a *death potential* within consciousness itself. To overcome this apocalypse humankind must heal this wound of separation and death and face its own destructiveness. The Tree of Life may then, in one sense, become possible—an extended period of time available to the human species. We face, therefore, the largest hurdle since the birth of our consciousness, the urgent overcoming of our destructiveness, selfishness, and "evil", which, if transcended, may allow us a new era and even to spread out beyond this planet. The fruit of the Tree of Life may be reached if we overcome the death potential in ourselves.

Trauma and hope

Humankind faces species-threat via a number of routes, including, first, the world economic machine destroying the ecology of the planet; second, the technologies produced by the Enlightenment and capitalist project destroying not only human civilisation but possibly all life on the planet. The conquest of the Great Mother, nature, becomes self-defeat.

Figure 31 is a representation of the apocalypse, taking as it motifs the nuclear bomb, the horsemen, and trumpeters from the last book of the New Testament, Revelation. At the centre of the bomb is the eye of consciousness, like Shiva, a creator and destroyer. Robert Oppenheimer, one of the "fathers" of the atomic bomb, on seeing the initial atomic explosion thought of Vishnu's words in the *Bhagavad Gita*: "Now I am become death, the destroyer of worlds". Later Oppenheimer was to warn: "If atomic bombs are to be added as new weapons to the arsenals of a warring world … then the time will come when mankind will curse the names of Los Alamos and Hiroshima. The people of this world must unite or they will perish."

Extinction threats are not new. Ninety-nine point nine per cent of every species that has evolved is extinct. There have been at least fifteen mass extinctions in the last 500 million years, roughly half the time since multi-cellular life emerged. In five of these fifty per cent or more of life became extinct in a short period. This can occur from meteorites, volcanic eruptions, poisoned oceans, methane eruptions, rising sea levels, and the like. However, there is a current extinction event on the earth but it is anthropogenic since it is humans who are now destroying the planet's life and can also terminate themselves.

A reduced impact scenario is that a proportion of the human race is wiped out and survivors reorganise their existence. This possibility is consistent with a harsh neo-Malthusian vision where the demands of the human race cannot be matched by the earth's resources or ecology. It is also strangely consistent with the Book of Revelation, where, after famine, plagues, wars, and the annihilation of a section of the human race, select survivors enter the kingdom of heaven as the chosen ones. It is quite likely that in the event of a mass extinction event, caused, for example, by nuclear error, terror, or warfare, that the conditions of the remaining survivors would be very primitive and precarious. An optimistic scenario is that a portion of the human race survive, for example, a whole country, and therefore possibly a civilisation, on a relatively isolated island such as Iceland, New Zealand, Madagascar, or on a whole continent such as Australia, with self-sufficiency, or something near it, already in place and surviving the terrible event(s). It is perhaps possible that such a reduced, fortunate, though traumatised population could reorganise itself in the light of a new vision of human existence. *Homo sapiens* may then avoid extinction but experience a death of at least a portion of its own species. That presumes, optimistically, that there will be survivors of the coming events. In other words, mankind must overcome death in order to pass to the next stage of its evolution, not just physical death but the death potential that is activated in its consciousness. Most of the paradigms that govern our collective existence, according to this radical position, will disappear—for example, that individual, separate nations are the natural or recommended way to organise the world political system. In the event of extreme events such as the above (which are completely possible now with our current technologies), global domination by one power might be the only way to survive—nationalisms would go into the dustbin of history and be regarded as primitivism. The idea that we will simply continue as we are, with our deep, destructive, compulsive economic greed on the one hand and our national chauvinisms on the other, is naive in the extreme. Nevertheless, self-renewal in this world is possible. It would, of course, be infinitely preferable that our species awaken to its imminent danger and change in the light of the knowledge available to us and to a new vision. This means that we might pass through the trauma of the near-death of our species to awaken to the simple truth that this earth is the most beautiful and wonderful mother we could have and that acting as delinquent psychopaths is no way to behave with nuclear weapons in our hands. In this life, in this fallen or separated state, we must overcome death, the terrible destructiveness in ourselves.

Jung commented that that which is not recognised within must be encountered as external fate. This psychological truth has to be extended when we deal with social, political, and economic systems. When we cannot take responsibility, as a society, for the destructiveness of our economic systems then we suffer the consequences externally—degraded environments, extinction perils, and warfare. However, we require much more than a change in attitude or belief. More than a realisation, we require an overhaul of the economic, political, and social systems that underpin, stimulate, and maintain our destructiveness. It is clear that practically no economy on earth is willing to forgo its obsession with economic growth, and since it is this growth that it is so destructive to the planet, then we must face the traumatic consequences.

While vested interests engage in outright denial, the global, educated community has known for some time the seriousness of the ecological crisis. Yet this information has been suppressed, ignored, or disputed. When reports of the oncoming ecological problems due to carbon emissions, largely from fossil fuels, *are* published they never persuade governments to actually reduce these emissions. No economy is going to leave oil, gas, or coal in the ground for the sake of humanity and forgo its own national interest in exploiting these resources. Our national economic systems are inherently self-centred and will only change if they feel some imminent threat to their own survival. However, this short-termism is of no use with respect to pollution, warming sea levels, greenhouse gases, and the like since these are long-term impacts on the environment. In any case, there is little commitment in even the short-term to reduce these pollution levels that are causing such severe ecological change.

It has been part of the argument of these pages that our consciousness, in the form of science and technology, serves our appetites in the shape of political power and economic greed. It is suggested, also, that we are not capable of deep learning except through harsh, even traumatic experience. No amount of theoretical knowledge changes our economic disposition to wreck the planet and destroy other life forms. There is a tremendous destructive aggression in the unconscious of our species that is directed to other human beings and to nature. Mankind, locked in fierce nationalisms, religious differences, competitive economic, and military systems, slumbers towards auto-annihilation.

It is said that Augustine was sweeping the floor of his monastery in Carthage when he was informed of the fall of Rome in 410 AD (the collapse of civilisation). Asked what he was going to do, he replied that he would continue sweeping the floor. While such equanimity may not be possible with respect to the events sketched above, a personal, individual quest for spiritual truth is the eternal prerogative of all mankind. To this topic we now turn.

Figure 31. The balance finely weighed.

PART VI

THE QUEST

If humans were to transmit into space only one essential image of the spiritual journey and a vision of our place in the cosmos, then the Shiva image, lord of the dance of creation and destruction, might well be it.

The circle of flames surrounding the dancer is the energy of the mass-energy-time continuum, the constantly evolving material universe; the hair of Shiva, the yogic knowledge of contemplation streaming to the edge of creation; the dance or *Nataraja* at the centre of material existence is that of creation and destruction, the eternal play of the cosmos, Lila, beyond good and evil. In the upper right arm is the drum by which existence is brought into being, in the upper left the flames that destroy it; in the lower right is the sign of acceptance—this is meant to be, the nature of things; the lower left points elegantly to the feet. The left foot is placed on the mighty dwarf, the ego which has to be overcome by higher knowledge; the right foot is raised against gravity by which freedom from this world and its opposites is achieved by the discipline of contemplation. Perhaps no other single image contains such total vision.

The individual quest for wholeness exists no matter what the state of the collective. However, the search for enlightenment is especially provoked by external crises in our societies and religions. The following pages are an allegory of this quest, presented as a pilgrimage. The pilgrim represents every woman and man who searches for the transcendent source of existence at the root of consciousness. The pilgrim has to battle through the cycles of creation and destruction to this higher awareness. There is an underlying template of psychological understanding of this process.

After the considerable difficulties of the preceding chapters, including the potential *inferno,* the reader is invited to enjoy the individual journey of The Quest, which is a *purgatorio* with a glimpse of the *paradiso.*

Figure 32. Shiva and the dance of creation and destruction.

The individual journey of The Quest

At the mid-life turning

At the mid-life turning
New compass may be sought,
Even your magnetic pole
May turn to south from north.
Your trade has been determined,
You've either lost or gained,
Reproduction's long been settled,
It seems life's played its game.

The autumn leaves begin to fall,
Summer blossom's done.
The joys of spring no longer yours,
Its seeds have flown and gone.
The powers of natural healing
Now begin to fade.
The body speeds towards its end,
You pass from light to shade.

A man within his garden sits,
The night sky starred above,
His family sleeps within the house
Protected by his love.
Life's tasks have been completed,
Success and failure mixed,
The moon shines strong in night's deep womb,
The soul awakens next.

Now he ponders on his life,
Darkling does he listen.
The sky upon its axis swings,
Beyond the tree moon glistens.
The stars revolve above his head,
In heart his fears rotate.
What meaning does his life still have?
What now will be his fate?

He soft surrenders to the void.
He looks up at the night.
"You're just a feather in the wind,
Put your perspective right.
You think you are the centre,
So many plans you've made."
A billion stars roll o'er his head,
Illusions start to fade.

Strong through the long night pondered he,
The moon passed 'cross the sky,
An intuition in him rose,
"Journey 'fore you die.
There's no more to accomplish,
Withdraw from outer strife,
Proceed upon a pilgrimage,
Make real your inner life."

Thus spoke a voice within him,
As whispers in the breeze,
He thought he saw an image in
The sky above the trees.
The stars they are a mirror,
We all see what we need.
Creation's force he dimly glimpsed—
The Sower and the Seed.

His soul fresh opened to the night,
A melancholy sweet,
That held him bound within her spell,
As when lost lovers meet.
The soul yearns strongly for her home,
She flies to stars from earth.
The mystery of the cosmos
She seeks her own rebirth.

Know that you are from the stars,
As well as from the earth.
The cosmos is a mighty womb,
To ALL it does give birth.

Figure 33. A man within his garden sits.

Comments on "At the mid-life turning"

Crises oblige us to re-examine our lives. In some cases this means reappraising the values that underlie our society. We may even revalue the foundations of our spiritual life. The journey from one position to another is here presented as a pilgrimage since it requires the leaving of the old self and searching for a transcendent source to our existence.

Islam requires that all believers visit Mecca at least once in their lifetime. India has many pilgrimage sites. The pilgrimages of the European Middle Ages are famous. Every civilisation has had pilgrimages in its tradition. These are natural spiritual phenomenon. The mid-life crisis, described by Jung, is a crisis of meaning occurring after earthly demands have been met—marriage, reproduction, economic security—and requires a search for deeper meaning. The increasing awareness of mortality occurs after the mid-life, typically when one's parents age and die and personal mortality becomes acute. The response to the anguish of death is the emergence of the higher self which may have been dormant up to this point but is now triggered into awareness. A pilgrimage is a journey whose end is to facilitate this connection to the higher self.

However, there are others who do not have to wait until middle age and, due to the nature of their suffering, are impelled to seek a spiritual source and meaning to their lives. They seek from an early age to cure the emotional wounds that have caused damage to their sense of self. The idea of pilgrimage may resonate with anyone suffering emotional or spiritual affliction. There are also those who are simply out of tune with the age in which they live and who need a deeper meaning to their lives than that provided by their society. The pilgrimage is therefore a metaphor for a spiritual journey to find ourselves and is a link to the divine. For instance, the Cathedral of Chartres in France, a famous pilgrimage site, has near its entrance in the nave a large labyrinth. Pilgrims arriving at the inspirational building are faced with the journey to their own centres.

The illustration and poem above show a simple event—the mid-life turning of a human being. Although in the security of land and home, although his trade is secure and his family have given him love, he gazes at the fire, into his depths, and contemplates his mortality and meaning. Many individuals, of course, have no such security and have to start from a far more painful position, but suffering is the fuel of the pilgrimage. Glimpsed in the starry sky is the image of the sower and the seed, a transcendent intuition into the nature of the cosmos and ourselves.

Separation

At dawn upon the rising sun
The pilgrim steps aboard,
A ship at anchor gently rocks,
Its cargo is fast stored.
The pilgrim on the deck looks out,
The night sky softly dies.
His family anxious wave him on,
Tears puzzled in their eyes.

Separation is an anguish
That haunts us birth to death.
Yet for the quest it is required
So we can find new breath.
Our mental state needs now to clear,
Detachment first we need.
If we're to find our centre,
The ego must recede.

This ego has attachments,
It seems they make our life.
The family is the matrix
For joy and for our strife.
There's love for those most near us,
Anxiety for their fate.
This is normal in us all,
Yet we must separate.

The ship at ebb tide anchor's raised,
The flags in winds high flutter.
Before her lies the open sea,
Behind her is life's clutter.
The pilgrim with the captain sails,
A friend long from the past.
For many he's a hero
Who's weathered storm sea's blast.

Sails are set to distant isles,
Where mountains touch the sky.
Since ancient times a pilgrimage,
Some in their heights have died.
His family watch him from the quay,
For good ship now they pray.
A shape, a mist, a dot, they wist,
Into the light it fades.

Now leave behind the life you've known,
its happiness and woes.
Your ship is poised, the anchor's raised,
out with the tide you go.

Figure 34. Now leave behind the life you've known.

Comments on "Separation"

The pilgrimage starts with the separation from the demands of everyday existence. The pilgrim leaves work, family, home, and friends, everything familiar to him. He casts himself into risk and some danger to reach a goal which has no material value but is a purely spiritual, inner potential.

The ego, our everyday conscious mind, is, among other things, a repressive apparatus enabling focus and concentration on a narrow range of the psyche especially concerned with planning and thinking. This is what allowed early humanity, vulnerable creatures, to survive. But as well as instincts and distractions the higher self is also filtered out or repressed. Spiritual consciousness requires that ego consciousness is no longer dominant. The ego is also the centre of our subjective sense of identity, the person I think am, the apparent centre to my personality. This, symbolised by the pilgrim's home and work, needs to be left behind. It is not abandoned but put aside temporarily so that a deeper level of consciousness may be accessed. This stage is therefore a separation from the ego and the world so as to give maximum chance for the emergence of the higher self.

As separation takes place feelings of previous separations may come to the surface, even the first of life, one's birth, with many of its powerful emotions. The final separation, death, is also constellated in the unconscious of the pilgrim. Awareness may emerge of a longing to heal the fundamental separation that lies in ourselves, that of our separated egoic beings, which long for unity with a transcendent self.

Storm at sea

Three nights upon their voyage
The pilgrim sharped from sleep,
Dreadful winds engulfed the ship,
The waves rose from the deep.
The captain at the helm stood firm,
The crew were strapped to mast.
The wind cried fierce a banshee's wail,
This storm would be his last.

Fast through the tempest terror struck,
A raging gale from hell.
A bird inside a hurricane
The vessel gasped and fell.
Storm-lashed on the open sea,
The stinging blast now roared.
The captain rode the ocean surge,
The waves like mountains soared.

The crew now prayed to God above
For mercy from the storm.
They cried forgiveness for their sins,
Some wished they were not born.
Colder grew the night and wild,
The gale still ran its course.
The bell it tolled "Lord save our souls",
The winds fresh gathered force.

Dark through night the tempest screamed,
The ship it still held bold.
The waters poured in torrents
Through decks into the hold.
She whistled by the rocks' sharp teeth
Sheeted like a ghost.
A lighthouse shrieked its warning,
Guns fired along the coast.

She shuddered like a terrored sheep,
The wolf fell on her neck.
The gale it howled and seemed to seek
The captain on the deck.
He stood amazed against the helm,
The waters round him roared.
A whooping billow dashed him then
Stone dead against the boards.

When storm had ceased the pilgrim rose,
Thanked God to be alive.
Many of that gallant crew
With their brave master died.
Despite the pain and anguish,
A voice rose from his chest.
"Consign the captain to the waves,
Continue with the quest."

Prepare yourself for life's cruel blows,
For shipwreck and for storm.
There is a light within you,
It's there since you were born.

Figure 35. Prepare yourself for life's cruel blows.

Comments on "Storm at sea"

As pilgrim leaves behind worldly connections he is more at risk. His support system diminishes and he is exposed. The storm poem represents these changes with the captain of the ship, an ego symbol, being the guide we hope to see us through the coming dangers. He represents the parts of the psyche that we have traditionally relied upon, our ego strength and valuable character traits, perhaps courage, intelligence, or determination. But at some point a crisis is reached when we feel stripped of our traditional defences and strengths.

Many people are struck by the storms of life: traumas and tragedies, perhaps the death of a loved one, or illness, betrayals and abandonment, the injustices of life. For some people their very birth or intra-uterine experience can be a trauma that shapes them for ever—their life is a continual storm. Others may have physical or mental illnesses that compromise the quality of life. One may ask, like Job in the Old Testament, if there is any meaning in such apparent cruelty and suffering. The friends of Job, following the Jewish faith of the time, insisted that he must have done wrong to deserve such punishment. The Karmic law of the Hindus similarly points to the actions of our previous lives as being responsible for the sufferings of our current life. But it is hard to contemplate that often that there is no cause of suffering that has any meaning, although there is moral, psychological, and spiritual consequence of suffering. In these pages we present it as a stripping away of the upper layers of personality and a bypassing of the ego, beneath which is the deeper self. The crisis reveals the structure beneath.

The captain's burial

The ship at shadow's anchor lies,
Its sails are draped in black.
The storm has passed, life's work is done,
He fears no more the wrack.
No more we'll see him at the prow,
Bracing winds demonic.
No more enjoy his subtle wit,
No smile was more ironic.

Suffered he a sharp dilemma,
Shone he like the sun.
Yet darkness his companion was,
His demons drove him on.
He would invite you in great style,
Tobacco he prepared.
At first entranced but then one felt
A knot of dark despair.

Fierce-charmèd was his presence,
It tempted you to love.
His mind was like Prometheus,
Who stole the fire above.
His wit did match Olympians,
From him came no repentance,
He'd tie you up in smoke rings,
Defeat you in a sentence.

And yet, so like a child was he,
At times, so innocent.
Who could guess beneath his charm
He had such discontent?

For vexed he was by many doubts
At the deep heart's core.
What in fact was his true worth?
What was his brilliance for?

All his life he sailed the seas,
By stars his ship did plot.
His wife did scarcely meet him,
His children knew him not.
He passed his years in search of gold,
Adventure he did crave.
His dreams were buried with him,
Beneath the ocean wave.

The ship at shadow's anchor lies,
Its sails are draped in black.
The storm has passed, life's work is done,
He fears no more the wrack.
No more driven by his fiends,
All is now full done.
The time has come, this sun has set,
Beneath the waves he's gone.

Cast into the watery grave,
All your dreams and songs.
Renew yourself in fathoms deep,
Now seek where you belong.

Figure 36. The ship at shadow's anchor lies.

Comments on "The captain's burial"

The captain of the ship, the ego and personality formation, is laid to rest. In the pilgrimage or transformation process this "death" is necessary so that the encounter with the deeper self can take place. The verse tells the story of a particular character, the captain, driven by opposites, brilliant but unfulfilled, outwardly confident, capable, and charming but suffering despair.

The old self with its defences dies so that a renewal or rebirth can, hopefully, take place. This is not only a spiritual journey but the everyday experience of depth psychology where the understanding and the by-passing of the ego and its defences are central to the growth of the individual. Defences are part of character formation. The ego not only defends against anxiety but also obscures the higher self. In declaring itself the captain of the ship the ego blocks access to the higher realm because it can only see its own reality. The ego and its defences need to be dismantled, to symbolically die, so that the deeper or higher self may emerge. The dreams and hopes that dominate this earthly existence die so that a new perception emerges, a different vision—a new person.

The spirit is the only force

Three long days and three long nights
The boat lay still becalmed.
The sails slacked low upon their rig,
As by a devil charmed.
The sea was like a level glass,
The heat hard stifled breath.
Fresh water gone the pilgrim prayed,
Since he was close to death.

The spirit is the only force,
The wind within the sail.
Without a muse I have no course,
My inspiration fails.
For all at once I am adrift,
No compass I possess.
My throat is dry, my soul is lost,
No words can I express.

But then she comes like summer's breeze,
So sweet the senses swoon.
She moves my heart, she gives me strength,
Her emblem is the moon.
The anchor's raised, the sails do stretch,
The barque flows sweetly on.
Pilgrim's at the prow once more,
At rising of the sun.

Figure 37. The spirit is the only force.

Comments on "The spirit is the only force"

The loss of the captain, the hero who has "weathered storm sea's blast", is a major blow for the pilgrim. Although he is at first determined to continue the quest he now stagnates. His spirit is gone, the sails no longer fill with the wind of inspiration; he collapses and feels close to death.

The transformation process is painful and once the ego's defences have been breached the underlying reality, parts of the psyche that have been long repressed, denied, or unacknowledged, now surface. In the case of our pilgrim this is the meeting with his shadow. However, his spirit returns and he proceeds on his journey.

The human personality consists of many parts. The search for integration, be it in the form of art, literature, architecture, spirit, or human relations testifies to the dissatisfaction with this fragmented state and provides the spiritual and emotional fuel for the journey of individuation or a greater integration of the whole personality.

The flow of the pilgrimage, its highs and lows, illustrates the variable parts of human nature. The illustration shows the pilgrim at the prow after the stagnation, isolation, and void within himself, an evolving personality who is beginning to understand that a new captain of the ship is required. This is the first sign of fresh vision, the new human being stripped of the old egoic layers of personality reorientating himself to the fundamental goal, the centre for which he searches. The sun and moon, prominent in the illustration, are references to alchemical motifs. They are masculine and feminine symbols, visually referenced in some of our illustrations. Just as the moon can be seen at dawn or twilight, the masculine solar consciousness at first needs to decline so that the feminine, lunar consciousness may emerge. This leads to the alchemical marriage of Sol and Luna, consciousness and the unconscious, the different parts of ourselves that seek integration in the new centre.

The dark night of the soul

Pilgrim lands upon the isle,
The world is far behind.
His life is left below him,
His soul he needs to find.
Renounced are his possessions,
His money now means nought.
He has the status of the wind,
He seeks what can't be bought.

In foothills of the mountains,
The pilgrim spends the night.
But shades of doubt assail him,
He fears he cannot fight.
"This pilgrimage is madness,
Do not risk the heights."
The voice of caution grips him,
"Here, you'll lose your life."

"This mountain is too high for you,
Climb it, you might die;
Spare yourself the torture,
This cup can pass you by.
Just contemplate the vista,
It's all within your mind.
Make peace with resignation,
Stay safe, remain behind".

Slow through midnight dark and long,
Despair the pilgrim gripped.
He cursed his life and its pretence,
With devil wrote a script.
He thought of life's betrayals,
And loves that had been lost.
He ate the dust of dark despair,
He counted out the cost
Of all that had been sacrificed,
And what he had believed,
How much he was a victim
So often been deceived.

But now the devil showed him,
By whom he was betrayed.
And who it was that most abused,
Of whom was he afraid?
"The source of all this evil,
This mirror can surmise."
The pilgrim looked in dark despair:
Himself he recognised.

The source of all this evil,
Within yourself it lies.
Look deep into the mirror,
Yourself now recognise.

Figure 38. The dark night of the soul.

Comments on "The dark night of the soul"

The mythical island is the deep self where the drama of transformation is enacted. Here, the old support system no longer functions; that which previously seemed important is no longer. One confronts the different parts of one's personality. The painful, repressed, and unacknowledged sides of oneself emerge and the mechanisms used to avoid them, for example, denial, repression, or projection, are no longer possible. With their energy exhausted, the darkness within the personality is encountered.

For the pilgrim, the ascent to the transformational heights now seems formidable and full of danger. He falls into doubt; the underlying shadow within and his despair emerge. Victim psychology overtakes him, the moment of truth arrives; he is forced to look square at himself and his own shadow. In the spiritual journey, and indeed that of psychotherapy, the meeting with one's shadow is decisive. No progress can be made unless it is recognised. It is very common for the shadow to be projected on to others. Its deep acknowledgement is an inner condition for the transformational energies to emerge.

The illustration shows an especially severe emotional condition. Self-destructive internal forces persecute the pilgrim and are tearing him apart. Such an affliction is associated with early childhood disturbance where abusive and traumatic conditions have been internalised in the helpless child and subsequently turn into self-persecution. Deep structural splits and divisions in the psyche require healing and are a great impulse for the transformational journey. Spiritual or religious groups that ignore this darkness and suffering within the individual can only provide superficial or defensive relief.

The poem tells the story of the search of the pilgrim and his meeting with the difficulties of the ascent to an integrated and higher self. At this stage, he is like a climber who has undergone great difficulties to reach his goal, has climbed a certain portion of the mountain and now faces the huge challenges of the summit. He falls into exhaustion, hopelessness, and even despair in every part of his being—body, mind, and soul. The pilgrim now hears inner voices counselling caution and the abandonment of the highest task. He at first falls into self-pity, resentment, and anger, believing he has been mistreated all his life. He then faces the moment of truth and realises he is responsible for all his own darkness. But can he face it? Can this dark vision be integrated?

The call of the sufferer

Horror now the pilgrim gripped,
It pierced him like a knife.
"I'm nothing but some vermin,
—Scarcely worth a life".
Bitter tears began to flow,
In depths of great despair.
He cried out in his agony,
His heart released a prayer.

Self-loathing is the greatest harm
Against that which is sacred.
It is a pain that can't be borne,
Deepest of all hatred.
Project it on to others?—
Destroy the life outside,
Internalise the hatred?—
This ends in suicide.
The other more creative route
Is that the pilgrim sought:
Descend into the darkest self,
Then seek the higher force.

"Save me Lord from such distress
This agony let pass.
My pride is gone, my life undone,
The devil's stripped my mask.
I yield unto your mercy,
I offer up my soul.
No one else can save me now,
Lord, please make me whole."

Eat the dust, all pride is gone,
The soul is in despair,
Self-loathing is the greatest harm,
Now you kneel in prayer.

Figure 39. The call of the sufferer.

Comments on "The call of the sufferer"

The point of greatest crisis is the opportunity for fundamental change. Unless this challenge is met the embedded structural defences of the personality stay intact. At the crisis the ego breaks or loses its coherence, and illusions concerning oneself fade. At this point the darker parts of the psyche may breach the defences and flood consciousness. There is no guarantee that the subject will sustain or recover from such dark invasion. However, a number of positive outcomes are possible.

First, there may be a cathartic reaction where a relief or purging is experienced by the open acknowledgement of these areas of suffering. One may realise that it is a means of progress.

Second, the dark areas of the psyche, traumas, and complexes, once their defences are non-operative, may reveal feelings that lie buried beneath. For example, below anger and aggression may lie sorrow and a wounded child. Reach the child and feelings may now flood in on the tears of sorrow.

Third, higher levels of the personality, unseen by the repressive and filtering light of the ego, may be reached, bringing illumination and integration.

The poem, following the self-persecutory theme of the previous illustration, takes one of the most serious of psychological afflictions—self-loathing. Again, it may arise from cruel parenting, where the child has been seriously abused and subject to intense and remorseless criticism. The hate of the parent is internalised by the child and becomes structurally built into the personality. It may also occur if one is forced by intense pressure and circumstances, such as those of warfare, to commit acts for which one subsequently loathes oneself.

At the darkest moment of the night, the *nigredo* of the alchemical process, comes the awakening of the third eye with its transformative illumination and intuition. The higher self awakens at the point of death of the defeated ego.

The illustration shows the suffering in depression, loss of love, and self-criticism, but it captures, at the moment of despair, the moment of the opening of an integrative, transcendental, higher intuition. An angel of these higher powers delivers this possibility; lunar consciousness awakens.

The pilgrim rises with the dawn

The pilgrim rises with the dawn,
He seeks the morning light.
But pauses then to recollect
The shadows of the night.
The time has come for wisdom,
To listen to the soul.
The parts of self must integrate,
So we become more whole.

He drinks the water from the stream,
And eats a crust of bread.
Nature like a vision seems,
He rises from the dead.
And life within the body
Returns like new day's dawn,
He feels there is forgiveness:
That he might be reborn.

Armed with the staff of healing,
The pilgrim now arose.
To heaven's light he raised his hands,
From lips these questions rose.
"The nature of the cosmos?
The pathway of the soul?
And that which we most long to know—
What will make us whole?"

And straight upon his anguish,
A voice there came full clear.
"This journey is your destiny,
The answer you will hear.
Have courage, rise unto the heights,
Your old self leave behind.
Through death's shadow you must go
A pathway you will find."

Figure 40. The pilgrim rises with the dawn.

Comments on "The pilgrim rises with the dawn"

The staff of healing carried by the pilgrim in the illustration shows the snake entwined upon it. This is the rod of Asclepius, the Greek god of healing, and bears witness to an ancient belief that the snake promotes natural and mysterious healing in the psyche and body. In ancient Greece healing temples or asclepeion were visited by pilgrims who sought emotional, physical, and spiritual healing. These temples or shrines to Asclepius were like alternative therapies clinics in which healing of many different types was found. Dreams and their interpretation were very important to the healing process and frequently the pilgrim or sufferer would stay at the asclepeion overnight where non-venomous snakes freely moved around. The dreams of the pilgrim, like in depth psychotherapy, would be of great interest to the physicians and guide the healing process. The snake symbol goes back through the Egyptians to the worship of the Great Mother where it was one of her animal companions. The serpent became a symbol of evil in Judaism and Christianity but this is far from the case in other parts of the world where it is associated with renewal, rebirth, wisdom, spiritual knowledge, as well as healing. The snake is clearly associated with the realm of instinct and therefore its worship points to a different value system to the Abrahamic religions. The rod of Asclepius in the illustration therefore indicates that underneath the Christian exterior of the poem, there is a wide and archetypal healing reference.

After the dark night of the soul there is the possibility of change. Within the darkness in the centre of the complex of suffering and negativity there lies an archetypal core of healing. When approached in the right spirit, as the pilgrim reaches the centre of the asclepeion, the voice within the darkness may speak. It may wish to be released or understood by the conscious mind of the subject.

With the emergence of light after the dark night of the soul, there is a burst of energy and healing. Integration of the darkness and light is now required. The pilgrim ascends the mountain in good spirits.

The vision of the sower and the seed

Three days and nights the pilgrim climbed,
He broke down many times.
As tears did flow his mind unhinged,
But truth began to find.
The first night in the mountain sky,
Creation's song he heard.
The source of all to him appeared,
He then did hear these words:

There is a sower and the seed
That's cast both far and wide.
Some of it has grown full strong
And some of it has died.
The field is rich and dark and deep,
It rolls forever on,
Each season is a cosmic breath,
Each flower a blazing sun.

In beginning is the light,
The Logos it is named.
And all the life of all the earths
Within it is contained.
And in the seed is spirit
With matter subtly mixed,
No man for all his wisdom,
Can tell how it is fixed.

Mankind is led by knowledge,
There's always more to know.
The universe beyond your lens
Forever seems to grow.
Within yourselves a spirit lives
It comes from far above.
Not only by intelligence,
It must be known by love.

And light combines with darkness,
As moon doth live with sun.
A marriage true that will not end
For life and death are one.
Within the seed destruction lies,
Each life has but one span.
And so it seeks to reproduce
In woman and in man.

The universe beyond you,
Above your petty fate.
For ever in renewal,
It's not early, it's not late.
It is eternal present,
The future and the past.
All within a moment,
It's neither slow nor fast.

The light within creation,
Lies deep within your soul.
It yearns for recognition,
It labours for its goal.
Patiently it works within
While generations rest.
A stirring seed beneath the soil
A pilgrim on the quest.

A million, billion, trillion times,
The square of billions more.
Is but a minute fraction of
The worlds the cosmos stores.
As droplets in the ocean,
And sands along its shore.
You live within the infinite,
But you are at its core.

The universe in Hindu thought
Has cycles like a breath.
Expansion is evolving life,
Contraction is a death.
There is throughout the ages
No beginning and no end.
Creation to destruction's wed,
Upon this wheel you're bound.

Intelligence is spread across
The cosmos far and through.
It is its very fabric,
It's all things and it's you.
So still the mind, let wisdom speak,
It lies within you all.
To be at one within yourselves,
And hear creation's call.

Figure 41. The sower and the seed.

Comments on "The vision of the sower and the seed"

The beautiful parable of the sower is from the New Testament and has fired the spiritual imagination for thousands of years.

> Behold, a sower went out to sow. And as he sowed, some seed fell by the wayside; and the birds came and devoured them. Some fell on stony places ... they immediately sprang up because they had no depth of earth. But when the sun was up they were scorched, and because they had no root they withered away. And some fell among thorns, and the thorns sprang up and choked them. But others fell on good ground and yielded a crop, some a hundredfold, some sixty, some thirty. He who has ears to hear, let him hear.
>
> (The New Testament. Matthew 13.)

While Christ refers to the spiritual message and how it is received, in these pages the image of the sower is used with reference to the cosmos itself and is a belief that life and intelligence have been seeded into it, that humans are not the result of accident but are a natural evolution from this cosmos. Consciousness is an integral evolution within nature. It is a belief in immanence, that the evolution of the cosmos has spirit and mind destined to evolve within it; that we are an expression of the evolving destiny of the universe. A child who realises she is wanted and loved feels totally different from one who feels her existence is an accident.

That the universe, or at least the earth, is the result of something divine has been the abiding conviction of all the world's religions and mystical thinkers. In an age that has discovered evolution, the theory of immanence suggests that spirit and matter are mixed together in evolution from the beginning. A more radical view, found in Platonic and Pythagorean doctrines, especially those of Plotinus, is that spirit precedes matter. In Hindu mythologies one also finds many references to the universe being a manifestation of consciousness or intelligence. This is a reversal of the assumption of modern science that consciousness arises from matter.

It is sometimes the case in psychotherapy or the spiritual journey that one symbolically "breaks down", losing one's way; one does not "know"; the old certainties disappear. This may be the precondition for the emergence of new thinking, energy, and inspiration from a deeper layer of the psyche; one admits that the ego is not in charge of the ship—so too, in our exploration of the cosmos. The findings of modern physics and cosmology are utterly astounding. We have knowledge that was impossible to imagine only a few decades ago. The advances have been breath-taking. Mankind pushes on for ultimate knowledge, the theory of everything, the unified theory, the ultimate particles. But this will evade us and we will reach a place in our knowledge of the cosmos when we say, once again, that we know so, so little and that we will have exhausted, at this stage, our struggle for knowledge; that this lens of our mind can only go so far—and be defeated. At that point the scientific paradigm will reconfigure and a new vision emerge, a new mythology that includes consciousness, ourselves, as a central part of evolution and the cosmos.

The soul's vision

The next day in the mountain,
Where light is sharped by snow,
A spirit strong enwrapped his mind,
More he wished to know.
The wind it quickened in the dawn,
The prophet in him stirred.
What is the nature of the soul?
These are the words he heard.

At end of life you might expect
To go before your maker.
That husk is sifted from the seed
Like wheat in field's full acre.
Winnowing wind the chaff may lift,
The essence is retained.
There's nothing left then to pretend,
The soul alone remains.

The seed that is your essence,
Of heart and spirit made,
This is what you really are,
A mix of light and shade.
This is what you have become
Throughout the course of life
Including joy and sorrow,
All your love and strife.

The heart has all the love you need,
How much you have to give,
So easily is it damaged,
To grow it must forgive.
Unless it frees itself from hurt,
It's trapped within its history.
Release the heart from painful wounds,
Unlock the healing mystery.

The spirit is your higher self,
Within the brow it lies,
Illumination of your path,
It shines as from the skies.
It lies above your petty fate,
Transcendence is the goal
The vehicle of becoming,
The guide that is your soul.

Death is construed in many faiths,
To be the final judgement.
The soul to either heaven goes,
Or hell to suffer torment.
Depending on the balance,
Your final fate is pending.
But in your ear a whisper comes
—"This is not the ending".

Destruction and creation are
The forces of existence.
The soul is milled as through a vice,
In death there's no resistance.
It then ascends towards the light,
The essence is revealed.
Some say the seed replanted is,
To grow in other fields.

For death the cruel destroyer is,
It reaps the harvest yield.
From out of death new life will come,
The seed is now revealed.
From out of death new life will come,
As day does follow night.
Transformation grips the soul,
It reaches for the light.

Now strip the husk, the chaff is gone,
The grain is left behind.
Seek for rebirth in this life,
The soul you need to find.

Figure 42. The soul's vision.

The goal of the individual

The final day in mountain height,
A voice rose from his heart.
The light grew strong in morning sky,
Soon he would depart.
A soaring question rose from earth,
It sky-flew like a bird,
How can humankind be whole?
These are the words he heard:

Five parts there are to humankind:
Your instincts at the ground;
Emotions and the ego next,
The unconscious then is found.
Though none should be neglected,
And all should have their role
But so that there is balance kept
Their master is the soul.

The instincts are your oldest part,
Evolved through countless years.
Desire and reproduction,
Aggression and your fears.
Totality of body,
A great deal of your brain,
Inheritance can't be ignored,
You're last link in a chain.

T'wixt creature and the ego,
Emotional structure lies.
Rooted in the deep earth's soil,
It reaches to the skies.
It's all your strongest passions,
The noble ones as well.
There has to be a guide for these,
Or you end up in hell.

The ego is the planning mind,
Dividing worlds in two.
First there is the outside,
Then inside there is you.
But ego's not the centre,
It serves that which you crave.
Alone, the ego's aimless,
It's only passion's slave.

The unconscious holds the shadow,
The parts that are repressed,
The person you're ashamed of,
It's this you should express.
For without this pain and anguish
You'll never see what's right.
Accept the darkness fully,
The burden then is light.

The still point of the turning wheel
Beyond the thinking mind.
A centre outside ego,
The soul's not hard to find.
It is a moral compass,
The logos and the means
To truth, to peace, to your core self,
The guide within your dreams.

"So still desire and aching mind",
A voice within did say.
"The grace of life within you dwells,
Let it have its way.
Through all your being let it flow,
Arising from the chest.
It pulses strong through all your fears,
Let peace be on your quest."

At still point of the turning wheel,
All motion is at rest.
Seek the centre of your self,
Let peace be on your quest.

Figure 43. The goal of the individual.

Comments on "The goal of the individual"

Pilgrim, like all humans, is divided into different parts, here characterised as a fivefold division: animal, emotions, ego, unconscious, and soul. The soul, otherwise here also termed the higher self, is the only centre that will give peace and integration to all the rest. The vision in the illustration is of an integration or wholeness that underlies the cosmos and human consciousness, so dominated by conflicts and opposites. Just as the world around us is full of variety and different forms, so too are our minds. As we sense that there is, nevertheless, a unity behind the world of nature, some integrative coherence underlying all the opposites, so we seek the wholeness that underlies the opposites that drive our psyche. The intuition that the universe and human consciousness are, at root, one, that they belong to the same oneness, will never disappear and is the root of all mystical experience. This oneness is the soul. It is *Brahman* in Hinduism, *Dharmakaya* in Buddhism, *Tao* in Taoism. Human beings, by the very nature of their consciousness, are aware that this state of division from the world, from other people, and within themselves, the conflicting parts of their psyche, is a state of alienation and unhappiness. The effort to overcome this state is intense—the desire for friendship, togetherness, to be unified in sexuality, to be one with nature, to be ecstatic, to love, to seek peace, to experience once again *participation mystique*, to break down the barriers of our consciousness. Many experience this in death. However, the disciplines of the East, and especially their meditative practices, have provided the most focused attention on this—the highest achievement of the human species, the realisation of transcendence, a deathless state of consciousness on this earth.

The goal of humankind

The fourth night in the mountain,
The pilgrim wished to find
An answer to a question:
The goal of human kind?
A storm now broke above him,
His spirit was disturbed,
He passed across a threshold,
These are the words he heard.

From out of earth your race arose,
From animals evolved.
With gift of reason you were blessed,
With soul you were endowed.
This paradise was given,
So that you could flower,
It's ruined by all this hatred,
Destroyed by seeking power.

When you awoke in consciousness
—Took apple from the tree,
From out of nature you emerged,
And broke its unity.
Arose you then as *separate* beings,
The first that did evolve
To search for your true meaning,
It's this that you must solve.

The darkness that's within you
Is all your greed and fears.
These instincts need to be transformed
Or this will end in tears.
The purpose of the human race
Is first to love the earth
Respect its living creatures
And know each other's worth.

You are the first to have a choice,
To know both wrong and right
The first to be aware of self,
To know both dark and light.
Your task then is to know yourselves,
Your shadow you must own,
Then integrate your instincts,
And listen to your soul.
For billions of experiments
Are in the universe,
Your earth is one among the rest
It's neither last nor first.
The human race from earth evolved
Till now it has survived.
This is the moment of your truth,
Your time it has arrived.

Your species now it must unite
And end its pointless wars
This surely is no way to act
With nuclear weapons poised.
Ambitions of the nations
Demand a heavy price
Your economic growth and power
Destroys this paradise.

Your ego is the prison,
Within it you're confined,
Controlled so much by passions,
By these you seem defined.
But truth lies far beyond these
Outside their narrow scope,
Unite with the intelligence,
This is the source of hope.

Raise your eyes to skies above,
The cosmos you will see,
The stars are sands upon the shore,
Within an endless sea.
This *plenum* it is seeded
With spirit far and wide.
There is a vast intelligence
That saturates the void.

Know that you are from the stars
As well as from the earth.
You are the living spirit
Of the universe.

Figure 44. The goal of humankind.

Return

The pilgrim to his home returns, so much remains the same.
People quarrel, people love, life still plays its game.
But now a spirit's gripped him,
His vision not denied,
The stars sweep high above his head
A dark glow in his eyes.

He says few words about the quest, his mutterings ignored.
Such thoughts are fit for crazy folk, the family seems quite bored.
They all continue with their lives,
Their troubles and their joys.
What else is there to talk about?
Please do not annoy.

The moon dance-dazzled in the sky, the wind leaved in the trees.
The air it sung a mystery, the sower cast the seeds.
The stars soft-pierced the dark night's soul,
Sweet anguish through them shone.
The cosmos on its axis rolled,
This life has come and gone.

The pilgrim lies besides the fire, his dog rests on the earth.
The wind soft whispers in the trees, there is both death and birth.
The pilgrim sees the sower cast
The seed across the skies.
The time has come, his life is done,
To earth he sinks and dies.

Thus passed our searching pilgrim, he went unto the earth.
The cosmos lives, the cosmos dies, forever it gives birth.
Millions more will follow him,
The spirit cannot rest,
It calls us ever to the light,
Upon the pilgrim's quest.

Arise and go now to your land,
Where there's no hail or snow.
Lay down your peace upon the earth,
You reap what you do sow.
Still the mind, quiet the soul,
Be one with deepest night.
Surrender to your destiny,
Rise into the light.

Figure 45. The Return.
Return unto your final rest, and know where you began,
Your life has come full circle, your birth and death are one.

APPENDIX ONE

Dating notation

mya = millions of years ago. kya = thousands of years ago. BP = before present.

BC and AD are used occasionally in the text although BCE and CE have become a popular usage—these new terms hardly solve the Christo-centric bias, however, since BCE and CE (*before common era* and *common era*) start the common era at the traditional date of Christ's birth.

Primate and animal inheritance

We share ninety-six per cent of our genes with our closest primate relative the chimp (*Pan troglodytes*). "Despite the similarities in human and chimp genomes … scientists identified some 40 million differences among the three billion DNA molecules, or nucleotides, in each genome. The vast majority of those differences are not biologically significant, but researchers were able to identify a couple thousand differences that are potentially important to the evolution of the human lineage" (*National Geographic*, August 2005). http://news.nationalgeographic.co.uk/news/2005/08/0831_050831_chimp_genes.html

The study on the link below indicates the existence of empathy, a sense of fairness and proportion, and an elementary capacity to calculate in chimps http://www.bbc.co.uk/news/science-environment-20973753

There is increasing evidence that self-awareness exists in certain animals, for example, dolphins and chimps. This was originally deduced from mirror experiments (the animal attempts to remove a mark on its face on seeing itself in a mirror) but has been extended to other more complex experiments http://news.discovery.com/animals/zoo-animals/chimpanzees-self-awareness-110504.htm

The Homo *genus*

The latest evidence (2014) indicates that *circa* 1.8 mya there were at least four identifiable species of hominids: *Homo erectus, Homo ergaster, Homo habilis* and *Homo rudolfus*, all in Africa. When our species, *Homo sapiens*, emerged later from this family line *circa* 200 kya, there were at least three other early human species: *Homo neaderthalis, Homo erectus* and *Homo floresiensis*. Our understanding of this family line will deepen as further evidence is obtained; this is a rapidly changing field. However, the broad picture that has emerged has become clearer. The human line emerged from Africa twice. The first was when *Homo erectus* left Africa around *circa* 1.8 mya and colonised parts of Europe Asia and the Far East. The second emigration was again from Africa, *circa* 70 kya, and within the space of 40 ky *Homo sapiens* was a global presence and other species of humans, especially *Homo erectus* and *Homo neaderthalis*, had disappeared. The picture we now have broadly confirms what we see in the evolution of many other species, where there is a simultaneous (and often competing) evolution of species within the same family group. The general pattern is that one or two survive to become a longer-lasting presence. Eventually almost all species become extinct.

Among the many remarkable features of this evolution of the *homo* family line leading to *Homo sapiens* is firstly the unprecedented speed of the evolution of the brain and secondly its extraordinary product, human consciousness, the subject of this book.

Some key dates

Homo habilis constructed stone tools—at 2.3 mya.

Homo erectus migrated out of Africa to large areas of Europe and Asia, including its colder regions—surely impossible to live in without fire and clothing—at *circa* 1.8 mya.

Hand axes were being used at 1.4 mya.

Cooking and hearths were used possibly 800 kya, certainly 400 kya.

Efficient small tools and weapon kits allowing hunting of dangerous prey at distance—400 kya.

Grindstones for plant seeds—280 kya.

Construction of dwellings—200 kya.

Symbolic forms of communication (the use of colour, incised symbols, decorative objects)—40 kya. (source: Smithsonian Natural History Museum)

Neanderthal burial

300 kya—first (disputed) evidence of Neanderthal intentional burial of the dead. Sites such as Atapuerca in Spain, with bones of over thirty-two individuals in a pit within a cave (Tattersal, 1995).

130 kya—earliest undisputed evidence for intentional Neanderthal burial at sites such as Krapina (Croatia).

There is evidence, therefore, for intentional burial of some Neanderthal dead, but there is little evidence for ritual objects within their graves. Tattersall (1995) concludes that this species did occasionally have burials but without the ritual and symbolic behaviour that characterised *Homo sapiens'* burial practices.

Intentional human burial

There is archaeological evidence for intentional human burial with symbol use at *circa* 100 kya at Qafzeh in Israel where "the remains of as many as 15 individuals were found in a cave, along with 71 pieces of red ochre and ochre-stained stone tools. The ochre was found near the bones, suggesting ritual. Ochre was often used in ritual processes by early Homo sapiens" (Smithsonian Natural History Museum) http://humanorigins.si.edu/evidence/behavior/qafzeh-oldest-intentional-burial.

Evidence of early care

The 530,000-year-old deformed skull of a child, found in Spain, indicates that some early humans must have nurtured and cared for disabled members of their tribe or family. This child, estimated to be ten years old at the time of death, had a debilitating birth defect called craniosynostosis, in which joints in the skull fuse before the brain has finished growing. The disorder increases pressure in the skull, impairing brain development. "It is amazing that this child was able to survive until 10 years old. This is the most ancient proof of social care of the handicapped," says Ana Gracia (2010), a paleoanthropologist based in Madrid, who published an analysis of the skull "Many mammals kill burdensome offspring," she points out.

Human evolution and ego consciousness

While the latest evidence is that *Homo sapiens* emerged in East Africa *circa.* 200,000 BP there is little evidence of the development of our species until *circa* 50,000 BP. Human population numbers were very low, sometimes at almost extinction level, and this is a small time-window to find solid archaeological evidence. Thus, we don't know, at the moment, at what point robust ego consciousness emerged. The likelihood is that *Homo Sapiens,* with his thirty per cent larger brain compared to *Homo erectus,* had significantly greater accomplishments in tool making, construction, weaponry etc., but that his ego consciousness developed over the next 150,000 years. By the Great Leap Forward of *circa* 50,000 BP it (modern humanity) is decisively present. At any rate, this is an extraordinarily fast development by palaeo-anthropological standards, considering the completely revolutionary potential of ego consciousness.

Evolution, physiology, and consciousness

The growing size of the human brain as we evolved from hominid to *Homo erectus* to *Homo sapiens* presented a serious anatomical challenge for the female pelvic canal. The baby emerges with a brain size thirty per cent of its later adult size allowing exit through the pelvis—a larger brain size would make this impossible—and greater room for cultural development of the infant since the brain grows and forms under the impact of a maternal and social environment. See: http://blogs.scientificamerican.com/observations/2012/08/28/why-humans-give-birth-to-helpless-babies/accessed 19 July 2014.

This makes the human infant uniquely vulnerable.

APPENDIX TWO

See: http://en.wikipedia.org/wiki/Timeline_of_evolutionary_history_of_life

In its 4.6 billion years the Earth has harboured an increasing diversity of life forms:

for the last 3.6 billion years, simple cells (prokaryotes);
for the last 3.4 billion years, cyanobacteria performing photosynthesis;
for the last 2 billion years, complex cells (eukaryotes);
for the last 1 billion years, multicellular life;
for the last 600 million years, simple animals;
for the last 550 million years, bilaterians, water life forms with a front and a back;
for the last 500 million years, fish and proto-amphibians;
for the last 475 million years, land plants;
for the last 400 million years, insects and seeds;
for the last 360 million years, amphibians;
for the last 300 million years, reptiles;
for the last 200 million years, mammals;
for the last 150 million years, birds;
for the last 130 million years, flowers;
for the last 60 million years, the primates;
for the last 20 million years, the family *Hominidae* (great apes);
for the last 2.5 million years, the genus *Homo* (human predecessors);
for the last 200,000 years, anatomically modern humans.

Periodic extinctions have temporarily reduced diversity, eliminating:

2.4 billion years ago, many obligate anaerobes, in the oxygen catastrophe;
252 million years ago, the trilobites, in the Permian–Triassic extinction event;
66 million years ago, the pterosaurs and nonavian dinosaurs, in extinction event.

Dates are approximate.

APPENDIX THREE

Commentary on text of Rig Veda

Then was not non-existent nor existent:
There was no realm of air, no sky beyond it.
Death was not then, nor was there aught immortal:
No sign was there, the day's and night's divider.
That One Thing, breathless, breathed by its own nature:
Apart from it was nothing whatsoever.
Darkness there was: at first concealed in darkness
This All was indiscriminated chaos.
All that existed then was void and form less
by the great power of Warmth was born that Unit.
Thereafter rose Desire in the beginning,
Desire, the primal seed and germ of Spirit.

Sages who searched with their heart's thought discovered
the existent's kinship in the non-existent.
Transversely was their severing line extended:
what was above it then, and what below it?
There were begetters, there were mighty forces,
free action here and energy up yonder.

Who verily knows and who can here declare it,
whence it was born and whence comes this creation?

The Gods are later than this world's production.
Who knows then whence it first came into being?
He, the first origin of this creation,
whether he formed it all or did not form it,
Whose eye controls this world in highest heaven, he verily knows it,
or perhaps he knows not.

Rig Veda, Hymn 129: Creation (Griffith, 1896/2009)

Note the vast speculative reach of the ideas, their sophistication and deep questioning. The poem contemplates the origin of all things:

The first quatrain (4 lines), *Then was not non-existent nor existent* ..., tells us that the origin *cannot* be described—they only say what it is not. The origins are beyond language and comprehension.

The second quatrain speaks, *That One Thing, breathless* ... of some singularity, some *one* that can, nevertheless, be said to exist at the beginning of everything.

The third quatrain, *All that existed then* ... describes, perhaps, the beginning of life ... the warmth and desire that lies at the base of it.

The next verse (6 lines), *Transversely was* ... shows the process of mankind's reflection ... *their severing line* is the dividing intellect that discriminates, analyses and judges ... this intellect speculates that surely there were some forces or gods that created this universe (the begetters and mighty forces). This quatrain ends by noting that there is free will here below with mankind, but up there, so to speak in the origins of creation, there is only vast energy.

The fifth quatrain, confesses in its first two lines, *Who verily knows* ... our inherent bafflement at the origins of creation. The last two lines, *The Gods are later than*, assert that the Gods come later than the origins of creation—very surprising considering that Hinduism is saturated in gods and goddesses. But this was also an idea that can be found in Egyptian mythology. Ra, the Egyptian father god, is not the ultimate creator of the universe although he does create the earth. He emerged from the waters (Nun), the unconscious, the primal oneness, as an egg.

The last quatrain maintains the enigma—with considerable humour.

APPENDIX FOUR

Standard model

The big bang theory of the origins of the universe has considerable evidence on its side. It suggests an original singularity followed by an immense, rapid expansion of the still expanding universe. Another account (without the same evidence) is given by Bohm in which a portion of the energy of the universe is converted to matter.

It has been estimated that ninety-five per cent of the matter in the universe is either dark matter or dark energy. Since energy can convert to matter then a "creation" or a very sudden event could happen, producing a vast amount of matter—that is, the material form of our universe. String theory, an attempt to unify quantum physics and relativity theory, hypothesises that parallel multiple universes exist. However, the evidence for this has not been found. The Planck mission team, using the standard model of cosmology, on a mass-energy equivalence basis, suggests the universe has 26.8 per cent dark matter, 68.3 per cent dark energy, and 4.9 per cent ordinary matter.

> *Empty space is full of immense energy and matter is a small quantised wavelike excitation on top of this background—a ripple on a vast sea. Space is full. It is the plenum of Parminedes and Zeno, the ground of existence for everything. What we perceive is derived from it. This plenum or sea is a vast multidimensional implicate order.*
>
> *The origin of our universe, the big bang, is really a little ripple—perhaps a wave pulse that explodes out with space enfolded within it. It contains relatively autonomous sub-totalities.*
>
> Italicised section abbreviated from Bohm (1980)

GLOSSARY

Abrahamic religions

The monotheistic faiths originating in West Asia with their roots in Abraham (Mesopotamia *circa* 2000BC). They include Judaism, Christianity, and Islam.

Archetypal realm

The area of the deep psyche, outside of the control of the ego, containing archetypes and healing intelligence.

Archetype

Inbuilt, psychic potential expressed in behaviour, thought, images, and creativity; universal in the human species.

Canaanite

The people belonging to an area that covers parts of modern Israel, Palestine, and Lebanon and in competition with Jews for land. Their religion was complex, sophisticated, and had many goddesses as well as gods—clearly felt by the Jews as a threat.

Capitalism

An economic system that developed from between the sixteenth to the eighteenth centuries AD in Europe, characterised by private ownership, the pursuit of profit, and capital accumulation.

Catholicism

A shorthand term for Roman Catholicism; those sections of Western Christianity with allegiance to the papacy.

Cave paintings

340 caves in France and Spain have been discovered that contain rock art:

In Cantabria, Spain, there are painted objects, including numerous hand-stencils and also abstract representations (dots, rectangles, and so on) that go back to 40,000 BP. However, the majority of painted figures and symbols date from 20–16,000 BP.
In Altamira, Spain, painted objects (chiefly animals) go back to 20,000 BP.
The Chauvet Cave in France has painted objects (chiefly animals) going back to 32,000 BP.
Lascaux is a complex of caves in south-west France, famous for its Palaeolithic animal paintings at 17,000 BP.

Chakras

Energy points along the central meridian of the body.

The First Chakra (base of spine)—connection to earth, security, foundation, and basic rootedness.
The Second Chakra (groin)—sexuality, partnership, and creativity.
The Third Chakra (solar plexus)—centre of will.
The Fourth Chakra (heart)—related to love.
The Fifth Chakra (throat)—expression, truth.
The Sixth Chakra (forehead)—illumination and intuitive insight.
The Seventh Chakra (crown)—the transcendent.

Collective unconscious

The deepest part of the psyche, universal in human species; referring to the higher and lower elements, instincts and archetypes, libido and healing intelligence, lower self and higher self (as conceived by Assagioli and Jung). It has multiple centres of healing intelligence as well as the central ordering archetype of the Self.

Consciousness

Concentrated intelligence in the brains of creatures, promoting their survival; evolving and manifesting from the inherent intelligence within nature.

Cosmos

The view that the universe is an ordered system. Pythagoras was the first to use this term. Also frequently implied is a divine intelligence that underlies or creates this order.

Creation–destruction

In Hinduism, the god Shiva is simultaneously destroyer and creator, portrayed as Shiva Nataraja (Lord of the Dance), which is proposed as the source of the notion of "creative destruction". In the nineteenty century it became incorporated into German philosophy, for example in the works of Herder, Schopenhauer, Nietzsche, and passed into Political Economy where it is implicit in the works of Marx (1988) and later explicit in those of Schumpeter who coined the term "gales of creative destruction" when describing capitalism thus:

> Capitalism ... is ... economic change and ... never can be stationary. ... The fundamental impulse that ... keeps the capitalist engine in motion comes from the new consumers' goods, the new methods of production or transportation, the new markets, the new forms of industrial organization that capitalist enterprise creates. ... The opening up of new markets, foreign or domestic, and the organizational development from the craft shop and factory to such concerns as U.S. Steel illustrate the same process of industrial mutation ... that incessantly revolutionizes the economic structure from within, incessantly destroying the old one, incessantly creating a new one ... Creative Destruction is the essential fact about capitalism.
>
> (*Schumpeter*, 1994, pp. 82–83)

Deep psyche

A parallel term to the unconscious and referring to its two components: the personal and the collective unconscious.

Disenchantment

The result of cultural rationalisation and devaluing of mysticism in modern society; used by Max Weber to describe modernised, bureaucratic, secularised Western society, where scientific understanding is greater than belief, where rational goals are dominant—in contrast to traditional society where, the utopian in him commented, "the world remains a great enchanted garden" (Weber, 1993).

Ego

It can be thought of in two ways: first, as a function of mind, providing a sense of planning, control, focus, and concentration; second, as the person one believes oneself to be, the centre of the subjective sense of identity, the experiential sense of coherence that is the centre of personality. Jung described it as the subject of consciousness.

Ego consciousness

A wide system of awareness and control at the centre of which is the ego.

Egyptian

Referring to Ancient Egyptian civilisation lasting from *circa* 30,00 BC to 30 BC before becoming a province of Rome; of importance in this book as a significant influence upon Abrahamic religions; although a patriarchy it had numerous goddesses. It is, in the view of the author, probably the best documented civilisation that has a strong link back to the older world of nature worship.

Evil

The destructive and life-extinguishing parts of animal inheritance as they pass through the potentially distorted lens of human consciousness.

Fallen state

In the Hebrew bible the state of mankind after being banished from Eden, separated from the creator. This was formalised by the Christian early church as a state of original sin passed on to the whole human race.

Fertility

Presented here, along with power, as a main creative feature of nature religions and the Great Mother.

Garden of Eden

The state of unity and harmony portrayed in Genesis as the original state of humanity before the fall.

Great Mother

A mother goddess, a divine personification of forces of nature, motherhood, fertility, creation, destruction; sometimes referred to as Mother Earth or as the Earth Mother.

Hero

An archetypal theme taken from Eric Neumann's book *The Origins and History of Consciousness*, in which there is a stage of the development of the psyche in which the ego and "higher" consciousness break from nature and the Great Mother to establish a new psychological world. See Neumann, 1989, pp. 131–169.

Higher consciousness

Transcendent awareness and symbolic communication over and above survival and ego needs.

Higher self

Used identically in this book to the term higher consciousness.

Homo sapiens

Evolved in East Africa *circa* 200,000 BP as an anatomically modern human. It was not until *circa* 50,000 BP that behavioural modernity emerged, evidenced, for example, by finely made tools, fishing, long-distance exchange among groups, self-ornamentation, figurative art, games, music, cooking, and burial.

Human nature

Here described structurally as having evolved interrelated layers: animal inheritance, emotional structure, ego consciousness, the unconscious, and a higher consciousness. These, we maintain, are held together by an intelligence, called by Jung the archetype of the Self, which is an expression of the integrated intelligence of the life process itself. Thus, human nature evolves from an intelligence that has evolved it.

Immanence

In this book it is linked to evolution and suggests that an intelligence manifests the material universe, which evolves into ever greater degrees of complexity and order in a process of creative destruction. The theory of immanence suggests that spirit or intelligence is within cosmic, planetary, and all life evolution; human consciousness is participatory in this unfolding. It contrasts with a notion of a static and personalised transcendent god who creates the world separate from himself. For an excellent account see Baring, 2013, p. 421.

Incest taboo

Claude Lévi-Strauss (1969) argued that the incest taboo was central to the structure of early societies obliging marriage and reproduction to be done outside of the immediate family structure. The evidence that incest is damaging both psychologically and biologically and that wider genetic matching between couples of differing genetic structure creates healthier populations is now overwhelming—quite simply, societies would not have developed without incest taboos.

Lévi-Strauss also points to this being the early basis of trade, gifts, and dowries. Social structure, repression, healthy societies, and economies are bound in a tight nexus.

Claude Lévi Strauss, as well as Freud (1912–13), proposed that an incest taboo lies at the root of the growth of civilisation. This taboo is reinforced with the advance of social structure, where greater division of labour takes place and more dense populations are created. In these, it is of importance that primitive instincts are controlled and channelled, that discipline is established. Thus, the questions of an incest ban, the importance of marriage and the like, become of vital importance. The unit of the family and its authority structure is seen as vital.

Individuation

Conceived by Jung as a four-stage development process in which first, the shadow, second, the anima or animus, third, the archetypal spirit, and fourth, the Self, are brought to consciousness; a process of becoming a more whole individual. It implies a release from the persona and over-identification with collective values and expectations. There is a continuous dialogue between ego and Self in which the centre of gravity of the personality moves from being initially centred at the pole of the ego to a midway position. Individuation is the natural development toward psychological growth and wholeness.

Inner awareness

A special portion of consciousness able to look inwards in a non-analytic, open way, uncluttered by regret, aspiration, or duty; a meditative-type skill, distinct from analytic self-reflection, it can access material from the deep psyche, facilitate its integration; it also possesses great healing power. This is not ordinary self-reflection but a special introspective function, a pure awareness of one's inner world. Its activation requires that other parts of consciousness, especially those of a judging, assessing, filtering, and analysing nature, are temporarily switched off.

Invisible hand

A term used by Adam Smith to characterise the hidden law of demand and supply determining prices by which all resources are allocated in an economy.

Logos

The Greeks Stoics (from the third century BC) used the concept of Logos as the animating essence of the universe. The Gospel of St. John names Logos (translated as the Word, but also associated with light) as the divine—"In the beginning was the Word, and the Word was with God, and the Word was God. He was in the beginning with God; all things were made through him, and without him was not anything made that was made. In him was life, and the life was the light of men. The light shines in the darkness, and the darkness has not overcome it" (The New Testament: John 1–5). There are numerous other references to the concept of Logos, chiefly in Greek and Latin philosophy.

Lucifer

A term used rarely in the Old Testament but meaning the morning light (or light bringer). In Christianity it later became identified with the devil (and Satan) who in the guise of serpent tempted Adam and Eve and caused the fall. In these page it is used as a symbol for the emergence of consciousness.

Neolithic

The last part of the Stone age, it was a period in the development of human technology beginning about 10,000 BC with the emergence of farming and ending between 4,500–2,000 BC; a period marking the rise of civilisations and the use of metals such as bronze and later iron.

New Testament

The Christian addition to the Hebrew bible. The Christian bible is both the Old and the New Testament. It serves as theological and moral teaching. It can be divided into four parts: the four gospels telling the life of Christ; the Acts of the Apostles; Epistles; and the Book of Revelation (end times).

Old Testament

Christian term for the Hebrew bible, written by many authors over hundreds of years, consisting of four parts: five books (Pentateuch) starting with the creation of the world; the history of the Israelites up to the Babylonian exile; the "Wisdom" books dealing with questions of good and evil; and the biblical prophets' books with frequent warnings to stay within God's law.

Origins of universe

The standard (currently prevailing) account of the origin of the universe is the big bang theory: that the universe was once a singularity and expanded extremely rapidly from a hot and immensely dense state. Alternative theories postulate the existence of many (infinite?) parallel universes, and/or the existence of infinite prior universes. A somewhat different account is given in Bohm (1980) whereby an implicate order (the underlying intelligence) manifests the whole material universe in an energy-matter conversion process—not so much a big bang as a "ripple" in the vast energy of the universe—see Appendix Four.

Palaeoanthropology

The study of ancient humans and hominids in fossil evidence such as petrifacted bones and footprints. Appendix One provides more detail.

Palaeolithic

The stone age, covering the vast majority of human and pre-*Homo sapiens* history, with three broad divisions: the Lower Palaeolithic, roughly from 2.5 million to 200,000 years ago, which includes pre-*Homo sapiens* species such as *Homo habilis* and *Homo erectus* who used chipped stone; the Middle Palaeolithic, the period from the emergence of *Homo sapiens* (anatomically modern humans) 200,000 years ago to roughly 50,000 years ago with *Homo sapiens* in a primitive state; the Upper Palaeolithic from 50,000–10,000 years ago when behaviourally modern humans emerged with a range of more advanced tools and equipment as well as international burials, self-ornamentation, painting, and symbolic objects.

Participation mystique

A term derived from anthropology and the study of early human psychology, denoting a mystical connection or identity between subject and object, or between human beings and nature.

> Mystical participation is an idea introduced by Lucien Lévy-Bruhl in 1910 to identify what it is about the mentality of so-called primitives that makes them understand things differently from Westerners. Lévy-Bruhl began his lifework as a professional philosopher in search of "unimpeachable truths" that would be universally human in their validity. To escape his own cultural limitations, he began studying the reports of missionaries and colonialists working among pre-literate peoples in Africa, Australia, the Americas, and Oceania—all baffled by what they took to be absurd beliefs on the part of the natives. Finding the same sorts of "absurdities" in all parts of the world, Lévy-Bruhl proposed that, while Europeans find meaning in events by looking for causal, empirical theories to explain what made them happen, "primitives" find meaning by seeing empirical events as "participating" in a larger, invisible reality.
>
> (*Encyclopaedia of Psychology and Religion*, 2010, pp. 667–668)

Participation virtuelle

An immersion or fusion of our consciousness with digital technologies and with artificial intelligence.

Patriarchal religions

Here referring to the Abrahamic religions who worship an exclusive, single, masculine god.

Perditio boni *(the destruction of the good)*

A term invented for this book indicating evil as the active destruction of the good, the life giving, and creative.

Pilgrimage

Presented here as journey to a sacred centre or transcendent source within the Self.

Privatio boni (*the absence of good*)

A term used by Augustine (354–430 AD) to define evil as an absence of goodness. It became Christian doctrine.

Protestantism

Branches of the Christian faith that broke from Roman Catholicism and papal control in the sixteenth and seventeenth centuries. In this text it is used with special reference to a tendency within it, especially Calvinism, favourable to some aspects of capitalism and democracy—as argued by R. H. Tawney (1880–1962) and Max Weber (1864–1920).

Psyche

The totality of the conscious and unconscious.

Psycho-somatic

The word psyche is taken from the Greek signifying spirit, breath, soul, or life, while soma signifies body or matter. Spirit and matter are mixed at the foundation of life and also the unconscious.

Repression

Freud in *Civilization and Its Discontents* argues for the inevitability of societal rules and repression of instinctual forces.

Revelation, Book of

Also known as the Apocalypse, the last book of the New Testament is a narrative concerning the end of time (envisaged to be imminent in the first century AD) and the ongoing struggle between good and evil. Of relevance to this book since the auto-extinction of our species is here contemplated.

Satan

Meaning adversary in Hebrew and identified as a malevolent force in the Hebrew bible. With the rise of Christianity Satan became a central figure against which the weight of the church was supposedly pitched. In this book the term is distinguished from *Lucifer* and is regarded as the *life-extinguishing*—the dark side of the creative-destructive polarity as it enters the human psyche.

Self

Referring to the archetype of the Self and in Jungian psychology conceived in two ways: first, as the totality of the psyche, conscious and unconscious; second, as the central archetype of order, an internal guidance system, orchestrating the development of personality. Jung thought of the Self as both an archetype and also the totality. In this book we use it in this dual sense also.

There is, then, ambiguity in the concept of the Self in Jungian psychology. Is it a component part or the totality? Is it a singular central archetype or the whole of the psyche? Although Fordham (1957) attempted to clarify this by defining it in the former sense, as the inner director, the organising principle, the archetype of order, I believe that Jung's ambiguous formulation of this archetype reflects something about its mystery. Much as the quantum world of subatomic physics indicates that one can't know both the location and velocity of particles (i.e., they have an inherent elusiveness and ambiguity—Heisenberg's uncertainty principle), so also, at the core of the psyche, there is a similar ambivalence. The Self has the capacity to manifest as both specific agent and the general totality.

Self-awareness

The development of consciousness particularly characterising human beings. However, it began to evolve in other species in the *homo* lineage, as well as existing to a limited, though definite extent, in certain animals, especially primates. It is the capacity of intelligence to examine itself.

Shiva

A popular Hindu deity and one of the five representations of the divine, possessing many forms, but the one of special interest in these pages is the Lord of the Dance of Creative Destruction.

Transpersonal

A term used by Jung and signifying the numinous, collective unconscious beyond the personal psyche with its complexes, traumas, neuroses, and personal history.

Shadow

In Jungian psychology parts of the psyche not accepted by consciousness; often mixed with shame or guilt, they are easily projected on to others. They compensate for ego ideals and higher parts of personality. This concept is of great value not only in personal psychology but also for understanding mass movements and radical, political group behaviours.

Spiritual

Here referring to an archetypal or foundational level—where the deepest human emotions touch the numinous and transcendent; also including the higher self and healing intelligence.

Tree of Knowledge

This the first tree in the Garden of Eden mentioned in Genesis (2:17) and represents the knowledge of good and evil. The forbidden fruit of this tree is offered to Eve who then gives it to Adam to taste. This leads directly to the fall. In this book this myth is treated as a commentary, in mythological form, of the birth of consciousness, which is a break from the primal unity. It is both an individuation and separation process of humanity as a whole.

Tree of Life

This is the second tree mentioned in Genesis (3:22); the biblical text tells us that it represents eternal life, no less, and this is the weightier reason why Adam and Eve are banished from the Garden; interpreted in this book as the possibility of enlightened consciousness for human beings if they overcome the death state of a separated egoic consciousness; it is also suggested that it represents something for the species as a whole, since if it overcomes its death potential (now actualised with modern weaponry) then a vast extended time for the human species becomes possible—eternal life?

Unconscious

The greater part of the psyche outside of consciousness consisting of a) psycho-somatic unconscious (genetic and neuro-chemical base underpinning all aspects of the psyche); b) personal unconscious (buried memories, defence mechanisms, complexes); and c) the collective unconscious (archetypal world bordering on instincts and the foundation of healing intelligence).

Yahweh

The name in the Hebrew bible given to the god of the Israelites—from the Hebrew word *YHVH* (from the Semitic root *to be*). In the early part of the bible God's name was also Elohim which may derive from the Hebrew *El* or *strong one.*

Yang

The masculine side of the rotating Taoist symbol of the Supreme Ultimate.

Yin

The feminine side of the rotating Taoist symbol of the Supreme Ultimate.

REFERENCES

Ambrose, S. H. (1998). Late Pleistocene human population bottlenecks, volcanic winter, and differentiation of modern humans. *Journal of Human Evolution, 34*: 623–651.

Aquinas, Thomas (2002). *Aquinas's Shorter Summa*. Manchester, NH: Sophia Institute Press.

Assagioli, R. (1965). *Psychosynthesis*. New York: The Viking Press.

Augustine. "What is called evil in the universe is but the absence of good" http://www.ccel.org/ccel/schaff/npnf103.iv.ii.xiii.html Accessed 10 August 2014.

Baring, A. (2013). *The Dream of the Cosmos: A Quest for the Soul*. Blandford Forum: Archive Publishing.

Baudrillard, J. (1994). *Simulacra and Simulation*. Michigan: University of Michigan Press.

Bekoff, M. (2000). Animal emotions: Exploring passionate natures. *BioScience, 50*: 861–870.

Bohm, D. (1980). *Wholeness and the Implicate Order*. London: Routledge.

Book of Job. Old Testament. Hebrew Bible. King James Version http://www.kingjamesbibleonline.org/ Accessed 10 August 2014.

Bowlby, J. (1969). *Attachment*. New York: Basic Books.

Bowlby, J. (1973). *Separation: Anger and Anxiety* (Attachment and loss. Vol. 2). London: Hogarth.

Bishop Usher. (1650). *The Annals of the Old Testament*.

Blake, W. *Illustrations of the Book of Job*. http://oll.libertyfund.org/titles/2155 Accessed 20 July 2014.

Blake, W. (1975). *The Marriage of Heaven and Hell*. New York: Oxford University Press, USA.

Bohm, D. (1980). Quantum theory as an indication of a new order in physics. In: *Wholeness and the Implicate Order* (Chapter Six, Part B, Section 5). London: Routledge & Kegan Paul.

Capra, F. (1975). *The Tao of Physics: An Exploration of the Parallels between Modern Physics and Eastern Mysticism*. Berkeley, CA: Shambhala.

Cashford, J., & Baring, A. (1993). *The Myth of the Goddess*. London: Penguin Books.

Cave paintings. http://www.lascaux.culture.fr/ Accessed 21 August 2014.

Durkheim, E. (1951). *Suicide: A Study in Sociology*. Glencoe, IL: The Free Press of Glencoe.

Durkheim, E. (1984). *The Division of Labor in Society*. New York: The Free Press.

Exodus, Book of. Hebrew Bible. King James Bible version http://www.kingjamesbibleonline.org/

Fordham, M. (1957). *New Developments in Analytical Psychology*. London: Routledge & Kegan Paul.

Freud, S. (1912–13). *Totem and Taboo. S. E., 13*: 1. London: Hogarth.

Freud, S. (1930a). *Civilization and its Discontents. S. E., 21*: 59. London: Hogarth.

Freud S. (1933a). *New Introductory Lectures on Psycho-Analysis*. Lecture XXXI, "The Dissection of the Psychical Personality". *S. E., 22*: 1–182. London: Hogarth.

Garcia, A. (2010). Humans took care of the disabled over 500,000 years ago. *Proceedings of the National Academy of Sciences*, March 2010. Reported in http://discovermagazine.com/2010/jan-feb/082. Accessed 21 February 2011.

Genesis. Old Testament. Hebrew Bible. King James Version http://www.kingjamesbibleonline.org/ Accessed 10 August 2014.

Giddens, A. (1991). *Modernity and Self Identity: Self and Society in the Late Modern Age*. Cambridge: Polity Press.

Gospel of St. John. New Testament. King James Version http://www.kingjamesbibleonline.org/ Accessed 10 August 2014.

Griffith, R. T. H. (translator) (1896/2009). *Rig Veda*. Santa Cruz, CA: Evinity Publishing Also at http://www.sacred-texts.com/hin/rigveda/rv10129.htm accessed 20 July 2014.

Grof, S. (1985). *Beyond the Brain: Birth, Death and Transcendence in Psychotherapy*. New York: State University of New York Press.

Haldane, A. (2010). The contribution of the financial sector: Miracle or mirage? At the Future of Finance Conference, London, 14 July 2010.

Hume, D. (2007). *Treatise on Human Nature*. Oxford: Clarendon Press.

Isaiah, Book of. Hebrew Bible. King James Bible version. http://www.kingjamesbibleonline.org/ Accessed 10 August 2014.

Job, Book of. Hebrew Bible. King James Bible version. http://www.kingjamesbibleonline.org/

Jung, C. G. (1973). *Psychology and Religion, Answer to Job* (Vol. 11, Collected Works). Princeton, NJ: Princeton University Press.

Jung, C. G. (2001). *Modern Man in Search of a Soul*. London: Routledge.

Kalsched, D. (1996). *The Inner World of Trauma*. London: Routledge.

Klein, M. (2003). *Envy and Gratitude and Other Works, 1946–1963*. New York: The Free Press. Also http://www.melanie-klein-trust.org.uk/ for concise account of key concepts.

Langer, W. C., R. G. L., Waite, & W. L. Langer (1972). *The Mind of Adolf Hitler: The Secret Wartime Report*. New York: Basic Books.

Lao Tsu (1997). *Tao Te Ching* (trans. Arthur Waley). London: Wordsworth.

Lévi-Strauss, C. (1966). *The Savage Mind*. London: Weidenfeld and Nicolson.

Lévi-Strauss, C. (1969). *The Elementary Structures of Kinship*. Boston: Beacon Press.

Marx, K. (1988). *Economic and Philosophical Manuscripts of 1844*. Amherst, NY: Prometheus Books.

Milton, J. *Paradise Lost*. http://www.planetpublish.com/wp-content/uploads/2011/11/Paradise_Lost_NT.pdf Accessed 10 August 2014.

Neumann, E. (1989). *The Origins and History of Consciousness*. London: Karnac.

Pitt-Rivers, J. A. (1954). *The People of the Sierra*. New York: Criterion Books.

Plutarch (1970). *Plutarch's De Iside et Osiride* (edited with an introduction, translation and commentary by J. Gwyn Griffiths). Cardiff: University of Wales Press.

Revelation. New Testament. King James Version. http://www.kingjamesbibleonline.org/ Accessed 10 August 10 2014.

Sallis, J. (1999). *Chorology: On Beginning in Plato's "Timaeus"*. Bloomington: Indiana University Press.

Savino, J., & Jones, M. D. (2007). *Supervolcano: The Catastrophic Event That Changed the Course of Human History: Could Yellowstone Be Next?* Pompton Plains, NJ: Career Press.

Say, J. B. (1803). A treatise on political economy. In: *History of Economic Theory, Vol 2: The Selected Writings of Adam Smith, Jean-Baptiste Say, and J. R. McCulloch*. Dublin, OH: Coventry House Publishing, 2013.

Schumpeter, J. A. (1994). *Capitalism, Socialism and Democracy*. London: Routledge.

Smith, A. (2003). *The Wealth of Nations*. New York: Bantam Classics.

Smith, A. (2010). *The Theory of Moral Sentiments*. Digireads.com.

Smithsonian National Museum of Natural History. Washington, DC. United States. http://humanorigins.si.edu/

Spikins, P. A., Rutherford, A., & Needham, H. E. (2010). From hominity to humanity: Compassion from the earliest archaics to modern humans. *Time and Mind*, *3*: 303–325.

Stoller, R. (1986). *Perversion: The Erotic Form of Hatred*. Karnac. London.

Tattersal, I. (1995). *The Last Neanderthals*. New York: Nevraumont Publishing.

Toynebee, A. J. (1939–61). *A Study of History* (12 volumes). Oxford: OUP.

Walker, A, Zimmerman, M. R., & Leakey, R. E. F. (1982). A possible case of hypervitaminosis A in *Homo erectus*. *Nature*, *296*: 248–250.

Weber, M. (1993). *The Sociology of Religion*. Boston, MA: Beacon Press.

Weber, M. (2003). *The Protestant Ethic and the Spirit of Capitalism*. Mineola, NY: Dover.

INDEX

Abandonment of religious outlook 149
Abel 100, 102, 104, 110–111
Abrahamic religion 52, 56–57, 71, 75, 80–81, 96, 105, 111, 118, 194, 224, 228
Adam 32, 78, 80, 84, 86–89, 95–97, 102, 104, 110, 137, 144, 156, 227
Animal inheritance 3, 16–17, 19–20, 70, 100–101, 118, 128–129, 211, 224–225
Answer to Job 56
Apep 47–48
Asclepius 194
Augustine 89, 116, 158, 229

Banishment 67, 90–92, 95, 104, 110
Baring, A. ix, xiv, 28, 37, 225
Baudrillard, J. 153
Behemoth 54–56
Blake, W. xiv, xviii, 37, 56, 86
Bohm, D. xiv, 13, 219, 227
Book of the Dead of Anhai 44
Bull fight xxii, 72, 75
Bull Worship 71

Cain 100, 102–104, 110–111, 120
Capitalism xiii, xv, xxii, 18, 132–135, 138, 140–143, 147–153, 222–223, 229
Capra, F. xiv
Cartels 132, 142
Cashford, J. 28, 37
Cave paintings 20, 28, 36, 76, 124, 222
Chakras 21, 124, 222
Chartres 166
Christ 59, 97, 198
Christian 53, 89, 96–97, 194, 222–223, 229
Christianity 53, 56, 67, 75, 82, 86, 92, 111, 116, 129, 194, 224, 227
Civilization 42, 68, 107, 110, 229
Collective unconscious 18, 20, 80, 222
Consciousness xiii, xv, xxi, 2, 12–29, 32, 36–38, 42–47, 50–57, 62–63, 65–71, 73, 75–77, 80–90, 92–93, 95–97, 101–104, 110, 116–119, 124–125, 128–129, 132–138, 144, 147–154, 162, 170, 182, 190, 198, 204, 206, 213, 222, 224–228, 230–231, 234
Consumerism 151
Corinthians 129
Cosmos ix, 2, 6–8, 12–13, 46, 52, 81, 124, 154, 162, 164, 166, 192, 196, 198, 204, 206, 208, 223
Creative destruction xiii, 42
Crete 73
Crisis 152, 166, 174, 190
Cybele 37

Daedelus 140
Demeter 37
Dragon 56–71, 75, 104, 118
Durkheim, E. 12, 149–150, 152

Economic view 133, 148–149
Education 133, 138, 150, 152
Ego consciousness xvii, 3, 17–24, 38, 75, 80–81, 89, 96, 100, 104, 117, 124, 170, 213, 224
Egyptian xiii, xviii, 29, 37, 46–48, 52, 66, 71, 100, 105, 109–111, 116, 194, 218, 224
Emotional structure 17, 222
Eve 78, 80, 84, 87–88, 95–97, 102, 104, 144, 156, 227, 231
Evil xxii, 52, 77, 80, 86, 89, 100–101, 105, 107, 109–111, 115–117, 128–129, 194, 228, 233
Extinction 97, 154, 156–157, 213, 216, 229
Ezekiel 53, 86

Fall 65, 77, 81, 86, 92, 102, 104, 115, 140, 158
Fallen State 66, 89, 95, 100, 104, 118
Fertility xxi, 29–30, 32, 34, 36–38, 51–56, 62, 70–71
Freedom 66, 68, 73, 75–76, 84, 104, 108, 133–134, 136, 138, 150, 162
Freud 24, 42, 75, 117, 226, 229

Galileo 134
Garden of Eden 97, 128, 158, 224, 231
Genesis 104, 110, 134, 224, 231, 274
Genetic bottleneck 42
Germany 43, 120, 147
Global expansion 137
Great Apes 16–17, 215
Great Mother xxi, 28–38, 42, 46, 50–57, 62, 66, 76, 89, 111, 156, 194, 224, 228
Grof, S. 43

Hathor 105
Hera 137
Heracitus 3
Higher consciousness 13, 20, 43, 100
Higher self 20, 25, 36, 75–77, 101, 124–125, 166, 170, 178, 190, 222, 230
Homo erectus 12, 20, 212, 228
Homo neanderthalis 12, 128
Homo sapiens xxii, 2, 12–13, 17, 24, 28, 36, 38, 42–43, 62, 64, 76, 87, 124, 128, 157, 212–213, 225, 238
Human nature xxi–xxii, 2–3, 16, 18–24, 29, 46, 82, 136, 138, 182, 225, 234

Icarus 63, 140–141
Ice-age art 128
Ideological justification 138
Immanence xiii, xiv, xxi, 12–13, 87, 198, 225
Inana 37
Individualistic 149
Inequality 142
Informational capitalism xxii, 152
Inquisition 119
Invisible hand 137, 142, 226
Isaiah 53, 86
Isis xiii, 37, 73, 108, 110
Islam xxii, 52–53, 67, 81, 89, 97, 105, 118, 166, 221

Job 29, 40, 50, 53, 57, 137, 174
Judaism xxii, 52–56, 86, 97, 105, 194, 221
Jung, C. G. ix, xiv, xvii–xviii, 3, 16, 56, 82, 120, 149, 157, 224–226, 230
Jungian xi, xiii–xiv, xvii, xxii, 2, 21, 82, 230

Kali 37
Kalsched 43
Klein, M. 42–43, 76, 104

Laussel goddess 128
Legalistic view 150
Leviathan 54–59
Lila 162
Logos 13, 196, 206, 226
Love xviii, xxi, 18, 20, 30, 37, 42, 48, 55, 73, 76, 78, 80–81, 95–96, 100–110, 117–118, 124–126, 129, 164, 166, 168, 174, 176, 184, 190, 196, 198, 200, 204, 206, 208, 222
Lucifer 53, 67, 80, 84–89, 104, 116, 118, 227, 229
Lunar 75, 95, 128, 182, 190

Maat 46, 110
Malthusian 157
Minos 140, 173
Minotaur 73

Mithras 74–75
Money 132, 142, 148, 150
Money relationships 150
Mount Tobo 43

Nataraja 162
Nazi 48, 120
Neolithic 76, 104, 227
New Testament 53, 129, 156, 198, 226–227, 229
Nibelung 47
Nigredo 90
Ninsun 37
Nut 37

Origen 19
Osiris 47, 71, 100, 106–107, 110–111

Palaeolithic 20, 36, 38, 56, 71, 124, 222, 228
Pandora 92–93
Paradise 67, 80, 87–88, 92, 128, 144–145, 154, 206
Parsiphae 73
Participation mystique 18, 20, 32, 34, 43, 76, 95, 128, 153, 204, 228
Paul 129
Perditio Boni 116, 228
Pharaohs 47, 107, 110
Plato 53, 81, 198
Plotinus 198
Plutarch 110
Power 32, 36–38, 53, 71
Price mechanism 137, 142
Private wealth 138
Privatio Boni 89, 116, 138
Prometheus 92–95, 176
Property Ownership 151
Protestant Reformation 147
Ptolemy 134
Purpose of human consciousness 3, 24

Reformation 147
Reification 151
Removal from nature 133, 148
Revelation 53
Rhea 37
Rig Veda 7, 13, 213, 218

Satan 53, 67, 86, 112, 116, 118, 227, 229
Self 6, 13, 20–21, 84, 117–118, 192, 230
Self-awareness 16–19, 86–89, 124–125, 211
Self-interest 125, 140
Seth 100, 106–107, 110–111, 120
Shadow xi, 19, 48, 58, 68, 86, 101–102, 110, 112, 115, 118–120, 133, 144, 154, 176–177, 182, 192, 202, 226, 230
Shiva xxi, 156, 162–163, 223, 230
Social transformation 137
Sol 182
Solar mythology 75
Sower and the Seed 164, 166, 196–197
Specialisation of knowledge 150–151
Standard model of cosmology 219
Stoller 119

Tauroctony 73
Technological transformation 132, 137
Torero 75
Toynbee, A. 73
Trauma xxii, 17–20, 32, 43, 67, 81, 87, 92, 104, 119, 128, 150, 156–158, 174, 186, 190, 230
Tree of Knowledge 80–81, 90, 96, 156
Tree of Life 80, 90, 95–97, 156, 231

Unconscious 3, 12, 18–21, 36–38, 55–57, 81, 87, 89, 116, 124, 150, 182, 204, 223, 225, 229–231
Uroborus 6

Wagner 47
Wealth creation 132, 142, 150
Weber 148–149, 223, 229
World domination 134, 139, 142

Yahweh 40, 50, 52–56, 71, 95, 165, 231
Yang 46, 231
Yin 46, 231

Zeus 92, 95

For Product Safety Concerns and Information please contact our EU
representative GPSR@taylorandfrancis.com
Taylor & Francis Verlag GmbH, Kaufingerstraße 24, 80331 München, Germany

www.ingramcontent.com/pod-product-compliance
Lightning Source LLC
LaVergne TN
LVHW080650011026
849160LV00014B/1375

9781782202462